W9-BWO-208

PETER REINHART'S
artisan breads every day

PETER REINHART'S
artisan breads
every day

Fast and Easy Recipes for World-Class Breads

PETER REINHART

photography by Leo Gong

TEN SPEED PRESS
Berkeley

Copyright © 2009 by Peter Reinhart
Photographs copyright © 2009 by Leo Gong

All rights reserved.
Published in the United States by Ten Speed Press,
an imprint of the Crown Publishing Group, a division
of Random House, Inc., New York.
www.crownpublishing.com
www.tenspeed.com

Ten Speed Press and the Ten Speed Press colophon
are registered trademarks of Random House, Inc.

Library of Congress Cataloging-in-Publication Data

Reinhart, Peter.
  Peter Reinhart's artisan breads every day / Peter Reinhart ; photography by Leo Gong.
      p. cm.
  Includes index.
  Summary: "Master baker and innovator Peter Reinhart's answer to
the artisan-bread-in-no-time revolution, with time-saving techniques
for making extraordinary loaves with speed and ease"—Provided by
publisher.
  1. Bread. 2. Quick and easy cookery. I. Title. II. Title: Artisan breads
every day.
  TX769.R4175 2009
  641.8'15—dc22

                                    2009021119

ISBN 978-1-58008-998-2

Printed in China
Design by Nancy Austin
Food styling by Karen Shinto
Prop styling by Harumi Shimizu

10 9 8 7 6 5 4 3 2 1
First Edition

CONTENTS

Where We Are and How We Got Here

For better or worse (and probably to your great relief), I am not going to rehash the extensive history of bread. It's a fine story and one worth reading, but authors like H. E. Jacobs have done that well (see the Resources section). Besides, I've already given a synopsis of the six-thousand-year history in both *Crust and Crumb* and *Peter Reinhart's Whole Grain Breads*. I believe what readers of this book really want to learn is how to make world-class breads quickly and easily. To accomplish this, we need only look at the discoveries and breakthroughs of recent years.

So here's a quick recap: The three waves that led to improved bread in the United States can be identified as the whole grain wave, the traditional wave, and the neo-traditional wave. The whole grain movement of the late 1960s was part of the counterculture era, in which white flour (and white sugar) symbolized industrialization and mainstream thinking, while whole grains became the symbol of a healthful, holistic way of life that had fallen by the wayside. During this period, organic foods were first promoted as an alternative to highly processed foods grown with chemical fertilizers and pesticides, ushering in what we now call the green movement. This whole grain wave introduced my generation to an alternative way of relating to food, but it took a few more years for dietary habits to change dramatically. Part of the problem was that most of the whole grain breads of that era, while nutritionally superior, weren't particularly delicious (or even palatable), so they came to be labeled "health food" breads, not fit for general consumption.

The 1970s and 1980s saw the emergence of the traditional wave, characterized by a culinary renaissance in which European chefs and bakers came to our shores. Likewise many Americans who exerted considerable culinary influence traveled abroad to experience the great food traditions of other cultures.

The third movement, the neo-traditional wave, grew from the second movement as regional cuisine in the United States became the local and domestic expression of traditional European and Asian influences. Bakeries applied classic techniques to create distinctly

American breads and pastries. At my bakery, Brother Juniper's, we applied slow fermentation processes to create breads using ingredients that would match well with the foods of the Sonoma County wine region or pay tribute to various other regional cuisines.

These three waves converged in the 1990s to create what is now known as the artisan bread movement. Meanwhile, many bread experts published books that shared their emerging and ever-evolving knowledge with home bakers, who were also growing in number. Bread machines helped fuel this trend, taking some of the intimidation out of the process. But more valuable, I think, was that Americans had finally experienced higher-quality breads, via restaurants and local bakeries, and they wanted to be able to replicate these breads at home. (This was also true of citizens around the world who were rediscovering their own country's bread heritage.) Every new book seemed to add yet another missing piece of the puzzle, and Internet discussion groups became abuzz with home bakers sharing their victory stories or asking for advice. Slow rise and slow food became a metaphor for better bread—and a better, more satisfying life in general. This era saw the inception of the Bread Bakers Guild of America and the international Slow Food movement, followed soon thereafter by the establishment of the Whole Grains Council and many other organizations promoting healthier, tastier, safer foods. The concept of a green lifestyle and cuisine finally spilled over into mainstream thinking, and, ironically, the best-selling bread book of recent times promised (and delivered!) artisan-quality breads faster rather than slower. The circle had closed.

Recently, I was asked to speak at a professional bakers convention on the subject of making artisan bread quickly and easily. My first reaction was that this seemed like an oxymoron. Artisanal methods aren't supposed to be easy; otherwise, everyone would already be using them. But upon reflection, I realized that this is already happening in the industry due to modern technological breakthroughs. Refrigeration didn't exist a hundred years ago, when bakers relied upon pre-ferments to extend fermentation time. Twenty years ago, we didn't have sensitive manufacturing equipment that could handle wet, sticky dough without damaging it. Only recently have American bakers grasped the biological and chemical processes of transformation that occur during bread making, the journey from wheat to eat, though there are certainly always new mysteries waiting to be unraveled. So perhaps it isn't an oxymoron at all, and given the new methods developed by other bakers and authors, and the public interest in new, streamlined methods, the time seems right for a fresh synthesis of all of the techniques that arose in the quest for the perfect loaf and loaves.

The past few years have seen the publication of a number of bread books that offer original methods for simplifying the bread making process. Yet during the same period, a few excellent books have appeared that reveal the advanced methods of true artisan bakers from around the world. We want it all: great bread, but fast and easy. Yes, it does seem like a contradiction since the premise of artisan bread is long, slow fermentation. Despite the often complex descriptions of methodology, bread making actually isn't all that difficult, so achieving the "easy" part is, well, easy. The "fast" part is where the challenge comes in.

Baking is primarily about the balancing act between time, temperature, and ingredients. Everything else is connected to this. In my previous books, I have taken readers on a journey in search of all of the workable variations on this theme of time, temperature, and ingredients. My goal in this book is to further synthesize that knowledge and apply it in a new way to create a system of baking that anyone can understand and perform.

In the following pages, I'll explain a variety of options for everything from pre-ferments to mixing methods to fermentation. In some situations, it's clear that a certain approach is preferable to achieve the desired results. While I definitely love exploring all of the options, you need to decide what works for you when it comes to balancing time with temperature and ingredients. What I intend to do in this book is funnel some of the newer baking methods and ideas through the structure of classic techniques and proven wisdom to broaden your sense of the options available to you. With each recipe in this book, I'll give a brief explanation of the thinking behind the method I've chosen. In some instances, I may present optional methods that require more effort or time in exchange for even better results. Many of the breads will follow the general method of a master formula, but not all of them will. Some of the formulas and techniques will seem familiar, while others may seem entirely new and perhaps unusual.

Chapter 1 explores the various methods chosen for this book, why I chose them, and what kind of results you can expect. It also includes instructions for shaping, mixing, and baking that will be useful throughout the book. Chapter 2 offers some fundamentals on working with sourdough and wild yeast. Chapters 3 through 5 apply the methods in chapters 1 and 2 to a broad range of recipes. While this book does contain some familiar recipes from my previous books, you'll also notice that I've included baked goods I've never written about before, such as Danish and croissant dough, rich coffee cake babka, and new holiday breads and crackers. Finally, in the epilogue, I'll take a look at what the artisan movement means to me.

Before moving on, though, I think it's important to remember that all of this growing interest isn't just a uniquely American bread revolution; it's occurring throughout the world, even affecting long-held French and German baking traditions and also reflected in the more recent Asian fascination with bread. The journey of discovery never seems to end. Though we've learned much about baking during the past twenty years, one of the most important lessons is that not only are there many paths to follow as we explore the realm of bread baking, but that new, unexpected trails continue to be uncovered every day. Forging one of these new paths is the task at hand—a path of fast and easy artisan bread baking. To locate it, we must look for ways to balance time, temperature, and ingredients that, somehow and against all odds, are not only easy and not only artisanal, but also fast. As you'll see in the following pages, accomplishing this means finding new ways to manipulate time.

CHAPTER 1

Baking Basics

The big breakthrough for U.S. bakers during the past twenty years was a new understanding of the relationship between time, temperature, and ingredients. Long, slow fermentation was first understood as simply a technique that made better bread. Later in the evolution of bread baking, we began to understand the actual science behind the various techniques. In brief, this science comes down to biochemical and biological activities that release trapped flavors. The activities are brought about by enzymes in both the flour and the yeast, and by microorganisms (bacteria as well as yeast) that create acids, alcohol, and gases. That's actually all of the information we need in order to set out on a lifetime pursuit of applications and variations, though many books have gone much deeper in explaining dough science and are worth reading. In fact, artisan bread baking could arguably be reduced to the following axioms:

* Use the best ingredients, including unbleached rather than bleached flour.

* Use only as much yeast as necessary to get the job done. Slower fermentation is better than faster fermentation.

* Mix the dough only as long as needed to get the job done to prevent oxidizing the flour, which bleaches the flour and reduces aromas and flavor.

- Use higher rather than lower hydration levels. More water equals better oven spring and thus bigger holes and better flavor.

- When shaping loaves, handle the dough gently in order to preserve the gases developed during the earlier fermentation cycle.

- Bake in well-insulated ovens at the appropriate temperatures. For crusty hearth breads, hotter and faster is better than cooler, slower baking.

- For hearth breads, large, irregular holes in the crumb of the loaf are preferable to medium, even-size holes. Larger holes allow the heat to penetrate more quickly to the center of the loaf, reducing baking time and preserving more moistness to create a thinner, crackly crust. Larger holes also indicate a better, gentler shaping technique.

Almost all of the bread books of the past twenty years speak to these points, and understanding them sets any baker well on the way to better breads. However, we are about to step beyond the boundaries of artisan orthodoxy and add some unconventional steps.

EXPLORING NEW METHODS AND TECHNIQUES

The use of old dough or pre-fermented sponges was developed by traditional bakers as a way of slowing down fermentation and, essentially, buying the dough more time to release its flavor (a result of starch molecules releasing some of their sugar and saccharide chains, as well as the formation of acids due to fermentation by yeast and bacteria). Some of these pre-ferments are wet and batterlike, while others are dry and firm; some are made with commercial yeast, while others use naturally occurring wild yeast (sourdough starters); some have salt, and some don't. What they all have in common is the idea of adding older, slowly fermented dough to young, freshly made dough to instantly age it so that greater flavor can be developed in less time. This is an example of the manipulation of time by the manipulation of ingredients.

Another way of manipulating time is by using more or less yeast, or warmer or cooler fermentation temperatures. One of the main functions of yeast is to raise, or leaven, the dough through biological fermentation, releasing carbon dioxide that gets trapped in the dough, pushing it up like a balloon. Both the amount of yeast and the temperature at which the dough ferments have a huge impact on the time it takes to raise the loaf. Typically, a difference of 17°F (about 10°C) will effectively double (or halve, depending on which direction you go) the rate of fermentation. Thus, dough that doubles in size in 2 hours at 70°F (21°C) will take 1 hour to double at 87°F (31°C) and 4 hours at 53°F (12°C). This doesn't apply to dough that's cooler than 40°F (4°C), where yeast goes somewhat dormant, or hotter than 139°F (59°C), where yeast dies.

Again, armed with just this much information, all sorts of permutations and manipulations of time become possible. Bakers from earlier baking traditions have come up with numerous variations in order to create distinctive regional breads, and within a specific tradition there may be numerous ways to achieve similar results.

Another lesson has been that in using this knowledge to produce more bread in less time by, say, increasing the yeast or boosting the fermentation temperature, we may get fully risen loaves faster, but often at the expense of flavor because the ingredients, especially the grain, haven't been given sufficient time to release their sugars and achieve their full potential. So the baker's mission, as I tell my students on their first day in my baking classes, is to learn how to draw out the full potential flavor trapped in the grain. I explain that the way to accomplish this is by understanding the effects of time and temperature on the ingredients.

All of this is a prelude to explaining the choice of methods used to make the breads in this book, many of which may seem to violate some of the axioms above. For instance, if the dough has been given sufficient time to ferment at a very cool temperature, it may be possible to increase the amount of yeast to boost leavening power and shorten rising time without sacrificing fermentation flavor. And because certain ingredients may dominate the subtle flavors that arise during long fermentation, extended fermentation time might not improve the flavor of the bread, even if the dough is held at very cool temperatures. In these instances, there's no advantage to long, delayed fermentation, but there may be ways to delay the fermentation anyway, in order to make the baker's work easier and faster on the actual day of baking.

The wild card in all of this, and the aspect of the craft that couldn't be anticipated by bakers of earlier centuries, is the invention of refrigeration. Controlling temperature is a very powerful method of controlling time and fermentation, and it has a huge impact on the ability of the baker to evoke the full potential of flavor from the grain. The baking community has only recently begun to explore the ramifications and options of this factor in the triangle of time, temperature, and ingredients, but this exploration has already led to a number of new baking techniques using refrigerated dough. This new method of delayed fermentation creates wonderful products, even from home ovens of less-than-stellar quality.

A NEW UNDERSTANDING OF DOUGH

I figured out the new methods for the doughs in this book by experimenting and testing old methods and conventional baking wisdom against new theories. For example, when I first read the instructions for the master hearth bread recipe in a recently published book, I immediately assumed, based on my understanding of dough science, that it contained way too much yeast to work as promised. How could it possibly last in the refrigerator for even one day without overfermenting while the yeast gobbled up all of the released sugar? How could it possibly create a tasty, moist, and creamy loaf (what some describe as the custard-like quality found in great breads)? Yet, when I made the recipe, it worked and didn't overferment. Sure, I saw areas where the recipe could be tweaked and improved upon, but this didn't diminish my astonishment at how greatly it exceeded my expectations. Although I have yet to find a scientific, chemical, or biological reason to explain why it works, the results forced me to reconsider all of the premises I once held sacrosanct. While certain scientific principles govern baking, one rule supersedes all others: the flavor rule; that is, flavor rules! In other words, if it works, don't knock it.

Some of the doughs for the recipes in this book are, by design, wet and sticky, and therefore tricky to work with. But this is one of the reasons the dough springs back to life so easily and well during the final proofing stage, creating fairly large, irregular holes in the crumb. You will also find options for whole grain substitutions in many of these formulas. As a general rule, you need to increase the liquid by about 1 tablespoon (0.5 oz / 14 g) for every 2 ounces (56.5 g) of whole grain flour you substitute in place of white flour. But even here, brands vary; you'll have to feel your way into it using the visual and tactile cues in the instructions as your guide. I've also included a selection of breads designed specifically as whole grain loaves, so in those instances you won't have to guess at adjustments.

I am indebted to the authors of other baking books using similar methods and have learned something from each. Still, there's always room for improvement. In these recipes,

What do you mean when you say the dough should be tacky but not sticky?

For some of the breads, especially rustic breads, the dough needs to be sticky to achieve a large hole structure. *Sticky* means that the dough sticks to a dry finger when you poke the dough. However, for the majority of the recipes in this book, tacky dough is the goal. Tacky dough behaves sort of like a Post-it note, sticking to a surface but peeling off easily. If you poke the dough with a dry finger, it should stick for a second but then peel off as you remove your finger. If the instructions call for very tacky dough, that means it borders on being sticky, so if a little dough sticks to your finger but most peels off, that's perfect. Once the dough chills in the refrigerator, it may seem less tacky or sticky because the flour and other ingredients have absorbed more of the moisture.

I've attempted to address and overcome some of the concerns I had after studying other techniques, especially to minimize overfermentation and unnecessary steps. I hope you'll find these recipes to be truly easy and consistently delicious.

Streamlining Baking: No Pre-ferments

Unlike the recipes in my other books, many of which required a *poolish* or other pre-ferment (usually made with cool water and fermented for many hours, chilled or not), many of the doughs in this book are made with warm water to encourage immediate yeast activity, and then refrigerated and fermented slowly. In some of these recipes, the dough is fermented a short while at room temperature and then goes into the refrigerator for cold fermentation overnight, or longer. In many of the recipes, the dough goes into the refrigerator immediately after the mixing stage; this way the dough doesn't develop too much alcohol or lose its ability to create a rich, golden brown crust. My most well-known bagel formula, published in *The Bread Baker's Apprentice*, used a *poolish* sponge as part of its method. The version in this book doesn't, making these some of the easiest bagels you'll ever make, yet the results are almost identical because of the overnight method.

In some instances, though, a sourdough starter (*levain*, or a wild yeast type of pre-ferment) is added to create a sourdough bread. Sometimes you'll have the option of using only natural, wild yeast *levain* or a combination of both *levain* and commercial yeast. Both are legitimate methods, each resulting in a different flavor profile. Instructions for making a wild yeast starter from scratch can be found on page 36.

Laminated dough, such as that used to make croissants and Danish pastries, is made using a cold, overnight method to improve flavor and oven performance. When using the method described in this book, there's no need for a pre-ferment, since the refrigerator does all of the work of manipulating time to achieve the full potential of flavor and texture.

Because rich breads, such as babka, brioche, and holiday breads, are loaded with fats and sugars that slow down fermentation, they require a much higher amount of yeast than lean hearth breads. Again, the balancing act between time, temperature, and ingredients is what determines the method. These rich doughs generally don't benefit from the addition of a pre-ferment, but I do offer the option of adding a sourdough starter to intensify the flavor and increase shelf life and moistness.

Some of the recipes include optional methods and leave some of the choices up to you. For example, there are many options offered in the bagel recipe: They can be shaped either on the day of mixing or on the day they're baked. There are two methods of shaping. Half of my recipe testers preferred one and half preferred the other. Try them both and see which works best for you. This was also the case regarding the poaching liquid: Some testers preferred using malt syrup in the liquid and some didn't. When it comes to bagels, one of those categories of bread where many strong opinions abound, I decided it was better to lay out all of the options and let you choose for yourself, especially since there was no clear consensus or definitive winner during recipe testing. All of the options worked, and each had fans.

Overnight Fermentation

In this book, I take advantage of a number of factors that aren't always available to commercial bakeries: refrigeration, small batches, and high hydration. For the most part, bakeries don't have enough room to hold large batches of dough overnight, so they use sponges or other pre-ferments to build flavor. But home bakers can, so most of the recipes in this book call for making a complete, single-mix dough, then using the refrigerator to retard the fermentation process. This gives enzymes and microorganisms ample time to work on the molecules in the dough and develop the flavor.

Is there a difference in performance between this method and methods that use a wet *poolish* or sponge?

Yes and no. In the hands of a master, yes, the acidity levels and leavening power of various pre-ferment methods can be slightly different. But if we distance ourselves from any loyalties to particular methods, we can see that the function of each of these pre-ferments is relatively the same: to produce a better-tasting loaf by evoking the full flavor potential trapped in the grain. While my previous books made extensive use of all of these types of pre-ferments, the recipes in this book use only one pre-ferment, sourdough starter, and even that in only a few of the recipes. Why? Because with the overnight method, the dough becomes its own pre-ferment through long, slow fermentation in the refrigerator.

Once the dough is mixed, in most cases it's quickly retarded to slow down activity of the yeast. One of the differences between this method and those I've used in previous books is that the recipes often call for lukewarm water (about 95°F or 35°C) rather than water at room temperature. This allows the yeast a chance to wake up and begin fermenting the dough as it cools down, until the yeast eventually goes dormant when the temperature of the dough falls below 40°F (4°C). A lot of the flavor transformation in the dough takes place during the dormant stage, because the starch enzymes are still at work even while the yeast goes to sleep.

The batch sizes of the recipes in this book are large enough to make multiple loaves. This is ideal, as the unbaked dough can be held in the refrigerator for a number of days, so you

Are there advantages to using a combination of pre-ferment techniques to achieve a better loaf, such as both *poolish* and *biga*, or *poolish* and sourdough? And what about soakers?

Sometimes yes and sometimes no, but it's hard to answer this until we factor in the third point on the triangle: time. When you really think about it, long, cold, delayed fermentation turns bread dough into its own *pâte fermentée*. In many instances, in fact, it may be redundant and not at all enhancing to add a pre-ferment to an overnight dough that undergoes delayed fermentation. Using a soaker, in which coarse grain is soaked overnight to induce enzyme activity and soften the grain, is an excellent method and perfectly appropriate in some recipes, but with the overnight cold fermentation in these recipes, this too is redundant because the dough serves as its own soaker, as well as its own pre-ferment. (That said, a few of the multigrain recipes still need and make good use of soakers.)

Can cold fermentation recipes be improved upon?

Yes, there's room for improvement, and this is where baking science can help. Applying the axiom of using only as much yeast as it takes to get the job done, hearth bread recipes (as well as many other yeasted breads in this book) either call for less yeast or shorten the first fermentation time in order to produce a dough that retains more of its natural residual sugars (released by the starches via enzyme activity). The result is a richer, browner crust and sweeter flavor.

only need to mix one batch to have freshly baked bread several times. Of course, if you prefer to work with smaller or larger batches, that's fine; just keep all of the ingredients in the same proportions.

A New Way to Work with Yeast

Another breakthrough method in this book is that of hydrating instant yeast, often using lukewarm water. Hydrating instant yeast in warm water is something I wouldn't have embraced previously, but I've discovered that waking up the yeast in lukewarm water allows it to ferment more effectively during the cooldown phase in the refrigerator. It also makes it possible to put the dough in the refrigerator as soon as it's mixed rather than having to wait for it to rise. The warmer dough and activated yeast have plenty of time to rise as the dough cools, so the dough is ready to use right from the refrigerator, without the wake-up time required in many of the other bread recipes I've developed.

Many brands of instant yeast are available to home bakers, under brand names such as Rapid Rise, Instant Rise, Perfect Rise, or Bread Machine Yeast. I've always liked instant yeast because it doesn't require hydrating in warm water (active dry yeast, on the other hand, must always be hydrated first). But for many of the recipes in this book, the yeast performs even better if hydrated in advance. Another benefit of this method is that it's the same whether you use instant or active dry yeast, though it's best to increase the amount by 25 percent if you use active dry yeast. (This is because 25 percent of the yeast cells are killed during the processing of active dry yeast, while instant yeast is at almost 100 percent potency.) Fresh yeast is wonderful if you can

get it—and if it's really fresh, as it only has a shelf life of 2 to 3 weeks. If substituting fresh yeast for the instant yeast, use about 3 times as much by weight to equal the leavening power of instant yeast. Fresh yeast should also be hydrated in water.

TOOLS: WHAT YOU'LL NEED TO GET STARTED

I strongly advise getting two tools if you don't already have them: a plastic bowl scraper (which is very inexpensive) and a metal pastry scraper (also called a bench blade, or bencher). I use these more than any other tools. An instant-read thermometer is also helpful in taking some of the guesswork out of the baking process. Parchment paper or silicone baking mats are also very useful, as are mixing bowls, measuring spoons, and measuring cups.

Mixers and food processors are useful but not essential. All of the recipes in this book can be made by hand, though a mixer will make the job easier. In many instances, I suggest finishing the mixing by hand even if you have an electric mixer because it's the best way to determine if the dough needs any adjustment with flour or water (and, frankly, because it feels so good—kneading by hand is the most therapeutic part of bread making, in my view). The brand of mixer is up to you, as all of them work to accomplish the three goals of mixing: even distribution of ingredients, activation of the leaven, and development of the gluten. Hands are also tools and can do the same, but a mixer is especially nice for larger batches.

You can also mix using a food processor; just be sure to use pulses, not long processing cycles, which overheat and overwork the ingredients.

Other tools that are useful but not absolutely essential include a baking stone for hearth breads, razor blades or slicing blades (*lame* in French) or a serrated knife for scoring the dough, a timer, whisks, cooling racks, and sheet pans as well as loaf pans. You might eventually want to purchase proofing cloths (*couches* in French) and baskets (*bannetons* or *brot* forms). But don't wait until you have these to start, as they can be approximated using tea towels, mixing bowls, and the like. Cloches (ceramic baking domes) are fun to use and make exceptional bread, but I haven't included instructions for using them. If you'd like to give one a try, you'll find plenty of information on baking with cloches on the Internet. Some of the

Common Questions about Ingredients

What about substitutes for milk, eggs, and honey?

You can always use soy milk or rice milk in place of cow's milk; egg replacers in place of eggs; and agave nectar (from the same cactus used to make tequila—it's delicious) or sugar in place of honey. You can use low-fat milk to replace whole milk, and yogurt to replace buttermilk, though you may need to thin it with a little milk. Another option for replacing whole milk is dry milk solids (DMS), using 1 part DMS to 8 parts water (by weight).

Why is unbleached flour preferable to bleached, and are there particular brands or types of flour that are better?

Unbleached flour retains the natural carotenoid pigments that occur in the endosperm of the wheat berry and give the flour its yellowish tint. Carotenoids also provide aroma and flavor to the flour and give the bread a more natural look. In rare cases, bleached flour is preferred (for example, for pie dough and biscuits) because it doesn't absorb butter as well, which helps create a more flaky, tender product. Other than in these cases, I always prefer unbleached flour.

As for brands, I don't have a favorite and have found that all of the U.S. brands of flour work well in these recipes, though some do absorb more water than others (the age of the flour is also a factor). The protein level varies from brand to brand, even among those labeled "all-purpose" or "bread" flour, so you may have to adjust the amount of water or flour accordingly. All of the recipes give cues about how the dough should look or feel and advise adjusting accordingly,

recipe testers reported making improvised cloches by using metal mixing bowls or roasting pans—creative substitutions are definitely encouraged!

I often suggest misting dough with vegetable oil spray, such as Pam or other brands, simply to make it easier to remove any plastic wrap used to prevent the surface of the dough from drying out. But a pastry brush and vegetable oil also work well, as do pump misters, which are now commonly available at cookware stores.

Finally, I highly recommend obtaining a small, digital kitchen scale. They have become fairly inexpensive and are much more accurate than spring scales or using volume measures. Most scales now also offer weights in both ounces and grams, which is very helpful, as grams are more precise. (The weights in this book have been rounded to the nearest measurable

rather than feeling bound by the amount in the ingredient list. Be aware that European flour is often different from American flour and usually requires about 3 to 5 percent less hydration.

Can I reduce the salt and how much should I use if I don't have table or kosher salt?

Salt is tricky because there are so many kinds, and their density varies. If you weigh your ingredients, it doesn't matter what kind you use; the ratio of salt to flour, by weight, will be correct. After all, an ounce of kosher salt is still an ounce of salt, even though it's made of much bigger flakes. But whereas 1 ounce of table salt equals about 4 teaspoons, 1 ounce of kosher salt equals about 6 1/2 teaspoons. To complicate matters further, different brands of kosher salt can have different flake weights. Morton's kosher salt (in two varieties) doesn't weigh the same as Red Diamond kosher salt. In this book, I'll give teaspoon or tablespoon amounts for both table grind and coarse kosher salt (based on Red Diamond, not Morton's). If you use Morton's coarse kosher salt, it's about the same as Red Diamond, but if you use standard Morton's kosher salt, in which the grains are only slightly bigger than table salt, split the difference between the two salt measurements given.

As for cutting back on salt, yes it is possible to do so; however, the bread won't taste as good. Another concern is that the yeast will have more leeway to ferment at will. (Salt is a yeast inhibitor, which is a good thing in breads.) So, if you cut the salt by, say, 10 percent, then also cut back on the yeast by the same amount. I'm not recommending this, because I like the breads with the amount of salt listed in the recipes, but I do understand that many people need to limit their salt intake. So as long as you're willing to sacrifice some of the flavor, you can make these breads with less salt.

unit.) However, the recipes do include volume measurements if you don't have a scale; just be aware that they aren't as accurate as weighing, since everyone scoops and packs ingredients differently, and because the density of ingredients may vary. For this reason, if you do use volume measures, be especially attentive to the visual and tactile cues I've provided so that you can gauge how the dough should feel and make any necessary adjustments.

BASIC TECHNIQUES

I've adapted and refined various baking techniques over the course of creating the recipes for this book. The new stretch and fold step, very popular now with professional artisan bakers, is probably the most exciting addition, but all of the other basic techniques outlined below are important for creating high-quality breads with the methods in this book.

Stretch and Fold

Stretch and fold is a method that makes it possible to use minimal mixing times even with doughs with high hydration. Some of the recipes suggest using this method to strengthen the dough and make it more buoyant. It isn't always required but if time permits, this will generally improve the performance of most of the breads in this book.

The key to the stretch and fold method is understanding that stretching out the dough and then folding it over itself helps organize the gluten network in much the same way as mixing does. Before using the stretch and fold technique, you must mix the dough until the gluten has formed. (If you need a refresher: Gluten forms as a result of the bonding of the proteins glutenin and gliadin, which are present in the endosperm of certain grains, primarily wheat and rye.) One stretch and fold is like mixing for another minute, yet it takes only a few seconds. As you use this technique, you'll immediately feel the dough strengthen, becoming a soft, supple ball. I have seen dough with over 90 percent hydration come together under the skilled hands of bakers using the stretch and fold method. In other books and recipes, you may see this technique referred to as turning and folding the dough.

To stretch and fold the dough in the bowl, with wet or oiled hands, reach under one end of the dough and stretch it out, then fold it back onto the top of the dough. Do this from the other end, and then from each side. Then flip the entire mass of dough over and tuck it into a ball. It should be significantly firmer than it was before you did the stretch and fold, though still very soft and fragile. Cover the bowl (not the dough) with plastic wrap and let it sit for 10 minutes, then repeat the stretch and fold process. Once again, cover the bowl and let the dough sit at room temperature for 10 minutes, then repeat the stretch and fold process twice more. The entire process should be completed in less than 40 minutes.

To stretch and fold the dough on the work surface, lightly oil the work surface and place the dough on it. With wet or oiled hands, reach under the front end of the dough and stretch it out, then fold it back onto the top of the dough. Do this from the back end and then from each side. Then flip the entire mass of dough over and tuck it into a ball. The dough should be significantly firmer, though still very soft and fragile. Place the dough back in the bowl, cover, and let it sit at room temperature for 10 minutes. Repeat the stretch and fold process, then return the dough to the bowl again, cover, and let it sit at room temperature for 10 minutes more. Do this twice more. The entire process should be completed in less than 40 minutes.

Shaping

After the dough rises overnight, you'll need to shape it before letting it rise, or proof, at room temperature. *Boules*, *bâtards*, and baguettes are examples of the most common free-standing loaves you can shape, or you can choose to bake sandwich loaves, pizza, or rolls.

BOULES (BALLS)

The *boule* is the fundamental shape from which many other shapes can be made. The whole process of giving loaves this shape is oriented toward creating tight surface tension, which allows the loaf to rise up and not just out; the tight skin causes the dough to retain its cylindrical shape rather than spreading and flattening. That's why the key step in making *boules* is to press firmly on the bottom crease to tighten the surface. This can be done in a number of ways, but the most common is to use either the edge of your hand or your thumbs to pinch the crease closed and exert pressure on the surface. If you look at the photographs with this understanding, with minimal practice you should become proficient.

To shape a *boule*, gently pat the risen dough into a rectangle, then bring all four corners together in the center. Squeeze the corners to seal them and tighten the skin of the dough to create surface tension. Use your hands to rotate the dough on the counter and make a tight, round ball. Flour a proofing basket (or line a baking sheet with parchment), then dust it with flour, semolina, or cornmeal. Transfer the dough to the prepared proofing basket, seam side up, or place it on the prepared pan, seam side down, to proof.

Transfer the dough to the work surface and dust with flour.

For lean dough and other wet dough *bâtards*, press firmly on the bottom crease to exert pressure on the surface.

For a lean dough *boule*, bring all of the corners together and squeeze to tighten the skin of the dough.

BÂTARDS (TORPEDOS)

A *bâtard* (literally, "bastard") is a torpedo-shaped loaf 6 to 12 inches in length. Aside from being a viable and popular shape in its own right, delivering a nice balance of both crust and crumb, it's also a good intermediate shape for making other forms. For example, rather than making a *boule* as a preliminary step in forming a baguette or sandwich loaf, I prefer to make a *bâtard* so that I'm already part of the way to the final shape. This way, less effort is required to finish the extension after a short resting period.

To shape a classic *bâtard,* gently pat the risen dough into a thick rectangle. Fold the bottom half to the center and press with your fingertips to hold the dough in place and seal the seam. Fold the top half to the center, and once again press with your fingertips to seal the seam. Roll the top half of the dough over the seam to create a new seam on the bottom of the loaf. Pinch the new seam closed with your fingertips or the edge of your hand to create surface tension on the outer skin, making a tight loaf. Gently rock the loaf back and forth to extend it to the desired length, typically 6 to 12 inches. To create a torpedo shape, taper the loaf slightly at each end with increased hand pressure while rocking the loaf. Transfer the shaped loaf to a floured proofing cloth or an oiled pan, seam side down, cover, and proof.

CLASSIC FRENCH BREAD *BÂTARD* SHAPING

BAGUETTES

The baguette is the shape made famous in Paris and is thus the ultimate city bread (as opposed to so-called country loaves, which are more round or oblong). The length varies from region to region, but for home bakers the determining factor is oven size. So even if you're able to make a perfect baguette shape as long as 3 feet, it's likely that your oven won't be able to handle it. For this reason, the instructions that follow are for 10-ounce (283 g) baguettes designed for home ovens and baking stones. Using a basic baguette shape, you can also create *épis*, which have a zigzag shape resembling a stalk of wheat. Since this is done just prior to baking, see page 30, under Scoring, for instructions on shaping *épis*.

To shape a baguette, start by making a *bâtard*, as shown on page 21, then let it rest for 5 to 10 minutes. Repeat the same folding process: bottom to center, top to center, and pinch to create a seam. Seal the new seam with your fingers, thumbs, or the heel of your hand. It should create a tight surface tension. Then, with the seam side underneath, gently rock the loaf back and forth, with your hands moving out toward both ends and increasing the pressure at the ends to slightly taper the loaf. Repeat this rocking as needed until the baguette is the length of the baking sheet or baking stone. Transfer the shaped baguette to a floured proofing cloth or pan, cover, and proof.

SANDWICH LOAVES

To shape a sandwich loaf, flatten the dough into a 5 by 8-inch rectangle. Working from the 5-inch side of the dough, roll up the length of the dough. Pinch the final seam closed using your fingertips or the back edge of your hand. Gently rock the loaf to even it out. Don't taper the ends; keep the top surface of the loaf even. Place the loaf in a greased pan, seam side down, cover, and proof.

PIZZA DOUGH

To shape pizza dough, press the ball of dough into a flat disk using your fingertips, then use floured hands and knuckles to gently stretch the dough into a wider disk. Work from the edges only, not from the center of the dough. Let the dough rest when it becomes too resistant, then continue stretching with floured hands and knuckles, again from the edges, not the center, until you have a 9- to 12-inch disk. Place the shaped dough on a floured or parchment-lined peel or back of a sheet pan. Patch any holes in the dough so the sauce and other toppings don't go through the dough. Add toppings as you like, then slide the pizza into the oven onto a preheated baking stone or the back of a preheated sheet pan. If using parchment, slide the pizza into the oven with the parchment, then remove the parchment after about 5 minutes of baking.

ROLLS

For round dinner rolls (also called silver dollar rolls): Place a 2-ounce (56.5 g) piece of dough on the work surface, cup your hand around it, then rapidly rotate the dough in a circular motion, as if trying to push it through the work surface. If need be, wipe the work surface with a damp towel to create traction to help you round the dough into a tight, smooth ball. Transfer the rolls to a parchment-lined baking sheet, cover, and proof. For pull-apart rolls, assemble any number of rounded dinner rolls on a parchment-lined pan, just touching, so they'll rise into one another. After they bake, the rolls will easily pull apart.

For knotted rolls: Roll 2 ounces (56.5 g) of dough into a strand about 10 inches long. Tie it into a loose single loop knot, leaving enough dough (about 2 inches at each end) to wrap around the strand one more time. Bring one end around and down through the center and the other end around and up through the center, so that a nub of dough pokes through the center on both the top and the underside of the roll. Transfer the rolls, nicest side up, to a parchment-lined baking sheet, cover, and proof.

Proofing

After the cold dough is shaped, it usually needs anywhere from 1 to 12 hours (as in the case of panettone) at room temperature to rise. This is called proofing, because it proves that the dough is still alive.

Slow rising is better, but sometimes a little prodding is okay. The main reason we can accelerate the proofing stage without harming the flavor in these recipes is because all of the flavor development already took place during the cold fermentation stage in the refrigerator. You can accelerate the rising process by placing the dough in a warm place, such as an oven with only the lightbulb on, an oven that has been briefly warmed and then turned off, or a gas oven with a pilot light. But if the dough warms up too quickly, the yeast ferments at a wildly uncontrollable pace. This can easily overferment the dough and ruin both the flavor and the color of the bread.

The safest way to accelerate the proofing is to use a warm oven but only for a short period of time—just long enough to take the chill off the dough without warming it. This is especially true of rich doughs made with butter, such as babka or croissants. The melting point of butter is between 80°F and 90°F (26°C and 32°C). If the dough gets warmer than this, the butter can separate out and ruin the dough.

The following are three common forms for proofing shaped dough:

BANNETONS

Bannetons are baskets used to provide structure for dough as it proofs. These bentwood baskets are much sturdier than wicker, but they are costly and, as with many other professional baking tools, can be improvised at home for far less money. With just a few basic items, spray oil being one of them, you can approximate many of the processes used in bakeries.

In this case, if you don't have professional *bannetons*, you can improvise with stainless steel or glass mixing bowls or wicker baskets. The size of the bowl depends on the size of the loaf, but since most of the formulas in this book are for 1- or 1^1/$_2$-pound (454 g or 680 g) loaves, the bowls need not be big. As a rule of thumb, the bowl needs to be twice as large as the piece of dough going into it to accommodate the rise.

Line a stainless steel or glass mixing bowl with a smooth, lint-free cloth napkin, scrap of fabric, or towel. Mist the fabric with spray oil, then lightly dust it with flour. Place the loaf in the bowl, seam side up, and mist the top with spray oil. Cover with flaps of the fabric or a separate cloth.

When the dough has fully risen, uncover the top surface, gently invert the bowl onto a peel or the back of a sheet pan dusted with semolina, flour, or cornmeal. Carefully peel off the fabric, then proceed with scoring and baking.

COUCHES

The same type of improvisation can be used for *couches* (literally, "bed"), the linen proofing cloths many bakeries use for freestanding loaves. If you don't want to buy actual heavy-duty *couches*, you can use a white tablecloth, preferably one that you no longer use for company! To prevent sticking, lightly mist the surface with spray oil and dust the cloth with flour before transferring your loaves onto the cloth, with about 3 inches between them. Once the loaves are on the cloth, bunch up the fabric between the loaves to make walls to support the dough, then cover with more cloth or plastic wrap. Proofing cloth is especially helpful with soft dough because the bunched-up walls prevent the dough from spreading sideways or flattening.

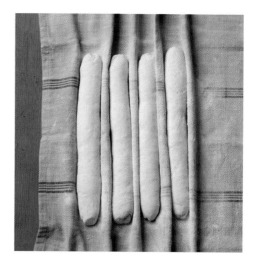

SHEET PANS

In truth, many of the doughs raised on cloth usually will do perfectly fine on a sheet pan lined with parchment paper, misted with spray oil, and dusted with cornmeal, semolina, or flour. You can loosely cover loaves on sheet pans with plastic wrap, or slip the entire pan into a food-grade plastic bag. Food-grade plastic bags, which are usually clear or translucent, are designed to store food without leaching any petrochemicals into it.

To use a sheet pan as a pizza peel, cover it with parchment paper so that the pizza will slide off easily; you will not need to flour the parchment or the back of the pan, but mist the parchment with spray oil in case you need to slide or move the dough after it touches down on the parchment.

Scoring

The purpose of scoring bread before baking is to release some of the trapped gas, which can make tunnels or caverns in the bread. This also promotes proper oven spring and creates an attractive finished look, so the cuts are both functional and aesthetic. Most of the time, cuts are made just prior to baking, after the surface has dried out a bit, but occasionally they're made earlier.

The most characteristic cuts are those associated with baguettes and other hearth-style European breads. They are best made with a razor-sharp blade, such as a razor or what the French call a *lame*, which is a double-edged blade on a stick. The cut is made with just the tip of the blade to avoid dragging the back part of the blade through the dough, as this would rip it rather than slit it. I often tell my students to say the word *slit* when they make the cut to emphasize an action like slitting open an envelope over any other notion of cutting. The cut shouldn't go straight down but rather be on an angle, so that it's almost parallel to the surface of the bread. This will encourage a separation between the crust side of the cut and the rest of the loaf, resulting in what is called an ear. As the loaf bakes, it will spring up in the oven, releasing some of the trapped gas through the cut areas, as they are weakest, causing the loaf to open into what's known as the bloom.

If you prefer to use a sharp serrated knife or another type of blade, remember to let the knife do the work. That is, resist the urge to press down on the dough. Instead, let the knife bite into the dough and then gently slide it through, letting the weight and sharpness of the knife do the cutting, rather than any downward pressure on your part. This will slit the bread more cleanly, allowing it to pucker open rather than collapse under the pressure of your hand.

To score loaves, wait until just prior to baking. If the loaves are in proofing baskets or bowls or on *couches*, gently transfer them onto a floured peel or the back of a floured sheet pan. Using a razor blade, *lame,* or serrated knife, score the loaf about $1/2$ inch deep. If using a razor blade, keep the back end up so it doesn't drag through and tear the dough. There are

Cutting an *épi* (wheat stalk).

Shaped and scored *fendue* (see page 33) and *fougasse*.

many pattern options when scoring, including a square, a pound sign, an asterisk, a sunburst, or parallel lines for larger loaves. These are just a couple of ideas to get you started.

To make *épis* (ordinary baguettes transformed into forms resembling stalks of wheat), use scissors to make a series of cuts just prior to baking. Starting about $2^1/_2$ inches from one of the ends, cut down through the top of the loaf and snip back toward the end at a 45-degree angle, cutting almost all the way through the dough. Turn the cut piece (the pointed end) to either the right or left, facing the point away from the loaf. Move down another $2^1/_2$ inches and repeat, turning the next piece in the opposite direction, until you reach the end of the loaf.

There are 2 methods for making *fougasse,* which makes a loaf look like a ladder or a tree:

Method 1: Use a pastry blade to slit open a proofed baguette just prior to baking it, then spread the baguette out flat.

Method 2: Flatten a proofed *bâtard*, then slit it with a knife in a pattern of your choice, spreading the cuts open just prior to baking.

Hearth Baking

A number of the breads in this book are designed to be baked at high temperatures, preferably on a hearth of some type. A baking stone is the most popular version for home hearth baking, but not everyone has one. In addition, a hearth surface, which is basically a thermal mass designed to absorb heat and then radiate it back into the dough, isn't enough if you want to achieve bakery-quality products. You also need steam to enhance oven spring and put a shiny, crackly crust on the bread.

BAKING STONES

I prefer the thick, rectangular stones now available in most houseware departments or kitchen supply stores. These stones retain their heat longer than thin, round pizza stones. The unglazed quarry tiles that many of us used before baking stones became widely available are also good, though they tend to slide around and are more prone to cracking when they get wet. If you've already outfitted your oven with tiles and are happy with them, feel free to continue using them.

If you don't have a baking stone, it's perfectly okay to bake on a sheet pan. The oven spring may not be as great, but at Brother Juniper's Bakery I baked my French bread on sheet pans in a convection oven for many years, and my customers loved it. Whatever works!

CREATING STEAM

There are many ways to create a blast of steam, including water misters and ice cubes on the oven floor, but my preferred method is to use a steam pan, either a sheet pan with a 1-inch rim or, as one of my recipe testers suggests, a lasagna pan with taller sides, or a cast-iron frying pan. Shirley Corriher, whose book *BakeWise* is one of my favorites, suggests putting stones in the steam pan to create more hot surfaces on which water can be instantly transformed into steam.

Both the steam pan and the baking stone should be preheated for at least 45 minutes so that they'll absorb enough heat. The location of the stone and the pan depends on the style and size of the oven. It's fine if the steam pan is above the baking stone, but in my oven it works best to place it on the shelf under the baking stone. Always use an oven mitt or a hot pad and wear long sleeves when adding water to the hot steam pan to prevent steam burns. It's also advisable to cover oven windows with a dry dish towel or rag to prevent backsplash from hitting the window and cracking it—but remember to remove the towel before closing the oven door! I use a watering can with a long spout when pouring the water into the steam pan because it gives me a little separation from the steam.

Why not use ice cubes? They do work and last longer than water, but you only need steam for about 5 minutes; after that it has done its job and it's better to let the oven dry out. Too much moisture in the oven after the steam phase delays caramelization of the crust, making it thicker and chewier. But another reason why I eschew ice cubes is that they drain heat from the oven. The caloric conversion for turning ice into steam is much greater than that for turning hot water into steam. Still, if you like the ice cube method, be my guest. Once again, whatever works!

To prepare your oven for hearth baking, preheat the oven with a baking stone and steam pan in place. Slide the shaped dough onto the preheated baking stone, then lay a kitchen towel over the oven's glass window to protect it from any potential backsplash. Wearing an oven mitt to prevent burns, pour about 1 cup of hot water into the preheated steam pan. I like using a watering can because of the control and distance the spout provides. Using a spray bottle such as a plant mister, you can also spritz the oven walls a couple of times to create additional steam.

BECOMING A BAKER

As you work with this book, you'll find that you need only a few basic recipes to give you templates for any number of bread variations. As with all of my books, one of my goals here is to empower you to think like a baker, not just blindly follow a series of steps (though following steps is also essential). Many home bakers have already made that leap, as witnessed by the stunning array of tips provided by the approximately five hundred recipe testers for this book. Quite a few of their tips and improvements have found their way into these recipes. In the pages that follow, you'll find a number of formulas representing various bread categories (lean breads, soft enriched breads, rich breads and holiday breads, laminated breads, sourdough, crackers, bagels, and more), along with suggestions for variations. Once you've learned these basic formulas, which are really templates for nearly every kind of bread imaginable, you should be able to create countless versions on your own.

I always encourage beginners to first follow a recipe as written, but it won't take long for even a beginner to start thinking of what-if possibilities, like "What if I substitute raspberry crème for cinnamon and chocolate in the babka?" Or, "What if I put a baking stone on the top and bottom shelf of my oven to make it perform more like a brick oven?" (A brilliant idea, by the way.) My answer to these what-ifs is almost always, "Give it a try!" In the end, the flavor rule (flavor rules!) will reveal if it works or not. In most instances, once you've made a particular recipe three times, you will own it and begin to think of your own tweaks and variations, at which point it will become your own personal formula. Don't wait for permission; trust your instincts and you'll soon be creating your own signature breads.

Remember, the basic methodology of this book is based on high hydration, delayed fermentation (aka long, cold fermentation), and only a short period of actual hands-on time. Are these recipes really fast and easy? They are easy—indeed, very easy—but they only appear to be fast. There's a substantial amount of slow work that occurs while you sleep; the fast part is the actual time you spend dealing with the dough. In some cases, there will be times of waiting, but in many of these recipes the waiting time for finished, delicious bread is minimal. As you learn the shaping steps, which are probably the most challenging aspect of this method, you'll begin to feel that no bread is too difficult for you to make (and rest assured that most of the shaping techniques take only one or two attempts to master). I predict that in no time at all, you'll find yourself on call for friends and family, baking for them again and again, as did many of the recipe testers while working on the recipes in this book. Now, on to the breads.

To shape a *fendu* ("split bread"), dust a *bâtard* with flour. Use a dowel, thin rolling pin, or a wooden drumstick to press a crease down the center of the dough. Using the dowl, widen the crease to make a 1 inch wide flattened area. Lightly dust the flat area with flour, then roll the halves back toward the center until they touch. Proof the dough with the crease side down for about 30 minutes, then flip it over and continue proofing, split side up, until read to bake.

CHAPTER 2

Sourdough and Wild Yeast Fundamentals

Many of the breads in this book require a natural starter, sometimes known as sourdough starter, in some cases with an option for also including commercial yeast. By sourdough I mean wild yeast or naturally leavened dough, as opposed to dough leavened with commercial yeast. Wild yeast breads have a number of appealing qualities, some related to flavor, and others purely romantic or philosophical. There's something compelling about capturing wild yeast and bacteria, then putting them to work to raise dough. It feels very craftlike and close to the bone. The flavor of these breads is often superior to commercially yeasted breads because, from the get-go, they require the use of a pre-ferment, called the starter. Since the starter has to be fermented in advance, it functions as a flavor enhancer, like other types of pre-fermented dough. But unlike pre-ferments made with commercial yeast, which have only a minimal leavening role, wild yeast starters also carry all or much of the leavening responsibility.

There are a number of classic versions of sourdough, under various names, that can be modified into many types of bread. *Pain au levain*, for instance, is a classic French-style naturally leavened (wild yeast) bread that's usually made with a small percentage of whole wheat flour but can also be made with 100 percent whole wheat flour or none at all, or with a touch of rye. The 4.4-pound (2-kilo) country *miche*, made famous by Max and Lionel Poilâne in

San Francisco sourdough (page 64), and pain au levain (page 61)

Paris, is made with sifted whole wheat flour. Sifting removes some of the germ and bran, but not all of it, so the bread is hearty but not overwhelmingly so. This can be approximated at home by using about 60 percent whole wheat flour and 40 percent unbleached bread flour. Traditional rye breads are often made with wild yeast starter to acidify the dough, which yields a better-tasting and more digestible rye loaf. Because rye is low in gluten, rye breads often include some high-gluten white flour to compensate for the lack of gluten. Many commercial rye breads are made using a mixed method that incorporates both a wild yeast starter and a commercial yeast.

BUILDING YOUR STARTER

There are many ways to make a starter, some more effective than others. You'll find numerous systems online, along with loads of information, misinformation, and folklore. Many people obsess over their starters, coddling them like newborn infants, keeping them on a regular feeding cycle, and fretting when the starter doesn't bubble up the way they think it should. Because there are many ways to create a starter, let's start by focusing on what a starter is and how it works.

The most common misperception about wild yeast or sourdough starters is that the wild yeast is what causes the sour flavor. Within the dough, there's an interesting microbial drama taking place. Wild yeast is living side by side with various strains of bacteria, and it's the bacteria that cause the sour flavors as they metabolize sugars and convert them into lactic acid or acetic acid. Different strains of bacteria create different flavors and aromas, which explains why breads made in different parts of the world may have different flavors even if they're made using the same formula.

From a functional standpoint, the role of the yeast is to leaven and slightly acidify the bread by producing carbon dioxide and ethyl alcohol, while the role of the bacteria is to acidify and flavor the dough and, to a lesser degree, create some carbon dioxide. This can be viewed as a symbiotic relationship, since the organisms harmoniously share the same environment and food source, and each supplements the work of the other.

In a best-case scenario, the acidifying work of the bacteria lowers the pH of the dough sufficiently to create an ideal environment for the growth of the desired strains of wild yeast. Of all the mysteries of bread making, this symbiotic relationship is perhaps the most fascinating. As the pH lowers to more acidic levels, commercial yeast doesn't survive, but wild yeast does. It all gets very complex, but fortunately this complexity manifests itself in the final flavor, as it also does in great cheeses and fine wines.

If you feel intimidated by making or using a sourdough starter, realize that it's simply a medium in which the microorganisms can live and grow in order to create their important by-products: alcohol, carbon dioxide, and acids. The job of the baker is to build the starter to a size that's capable of raising the dough. Combining the delayed fermentation method used in this book with the complexity that a wild yeast starter brings to the dough allows us to create extremely tasty dough with many layers of flavor—or, as one of my students calls it, "Bread to the max!"

First Stage: The Seed Culture

This starter comes together in two stages: first, you'll create the seed culture, then you'll convert it to a mother starter. In the first stage, you aren't making the starter that actually goes into your dough; you're making a starter (the seed) that makes another starter (the mother), from which you'll make your final dough.

There are many ways to make a seed culture. The simplest is with just flour and water. This does work, but not always on a predictable schedule. I've seen methods on the Internet calling for onion skins, wine grapes, plums, potatoes, milk, buttermilk, and yogurt. These can all serve as fuel for the microorganisms, and all of them also work for making a seed culture. But ultimately, a starter (and bread itself) is really about fermented flour. So in this book the goal is to create the conditions in which the appropriate organisms can grow and thrive so that they can create great-tasting bread.

The following method produces a versatile starter that can be used to make 100 percent sourdough breads as well as mixed-method breads (breads leavened with a combination of wild yeast starter and commercial yeast). However, if you already have a starter or used a different method to make a starter, feel free to use it. The starter can be made from whole wheat flour, unbleached white bread flour, or whole rye flour. (Rye bread fanatics tend to keep a rye-only starter, but in my opinion a wheat starter works just as well in rye breads.) If you already have a finished starter, whether whole grain or white, it can be used as the mother starter for any of the formulas in this book, as directed in the various recipes.

You may wonder about the inclusion of pineapple juice in the early stages of making the seed starter. Pineapple juice neutralizes a dastardly bacteria that can sabotage your starter (this bacteria, leuconostoc, has been showing up more often in flour and I have written about it extensively on my blog; see Resources, page 205). If you're the mad scientist type, as so many bread baking enthusiasts are, feel free to experiment with other acids, such as ascorbic acid or citric acid, as in orange juice or lemon juice.

One final word of advice: If your seed culture doesn't respond in exactly the way described, on the exact schedule predicted, just give it more time. In most instances, the good microbial guys eventually prevail, allowing the seed to thrive and fulfill its mission.

Seed Culture, Phase 1 (Day 1)

3¹/₂ tablespoons (1 oz / 28.5 g) whole wheat flour, whole rye flour, or unbleached bread flour

¹/₄ cup (2 oz / 56.5 g) unsweetened pineapple juice, filtered water, or spring water

In a small nonreactive bowl or 2-cup glass measuring cup, stir the flour and juice together with a spoon or whisk to make a paste or sponge with the consistency of thin pancake batter. Make sure all of the flour is hydrated. (Transfer the remaining juice into a clean jar and refrigerate it; or just go ahead and drink it.) Cover the bowl with plastic wrap and leave it at room temperature for 48 hours. Two to three times each day, stir the seed culture for about 10 seconds with a wet spoon or whisk to aerate it. There will be few or no bubbles (indicating fermentation activity) during the first 24 hours, but bubbles may begin to appear within 48 hours.

Seed Culture, Phase 2 (Day 3)

3¹/₂ tablespoons (1 oz / 28.5 g) whole wheat flour, whole rye flour, or unbleached bread flour

2 tablespoons (1 oz / 28.5 g) unsweetened pineapple juice, filtered water, or spring water

All of the Phase 1 seed culture (3 oz / 85 g)

Add the new ingredients to the Phase 1 seed culture and stir with a spoon or whisk to distribute and fully hydrate the new flour. (The liquid can be cold or at room temperature; it doesn't matter.) Again, cover with plastic wrap and leave at room temperature for 24 to 48 hours, stirring with a wet spoon or whisk to aerate two or three times each day. There should be signs of fermentation (bubbling and growth) during this period. When the culture becomes very bubbly or foamy, continue to Phase 3. This phase could take anywhere from 1 to 4 days. As long as you aerate the seed culture regularly, it will not spoil or develop mold.

Seed Culture, Phase 3 (Day 4 or Later)

7 tablespoons (2 oz / 56.5 g) whole wheat flour, whole rye flour, or unbleached bread flour

2 tablespoons (1 oz / 28.5 g) filtered or spring water

All of the Phase 2 seed culture (5 oz / 142 g)

Add the new ingredients to the now bubbling Phase 2 seed culture and stir with a spoon or whisk as before, or knead by hand. (The seed culture will be thicker because the the ratio of liquid to flour has decreased with each addition.) Place it in a larger bowl or measuring cup, cover with plastic wrap, and leave at room temperature for 24 to 48 hours, aerating with a wet spoon or whisk (or knead with wet hands) at least twice each day. Within 48 hours the culture should be very bubbly and expanded. If not, wait another day or two, continuing to aerate at least twice a day, until it becomes active and doubles in size. (If the seed culture was active and bubbly prior to entering this phase, it could become active and bubbly in this stage in less than 24 hours. If so, proceed to the next phase as soon as that happens.)

Seed Culture, Phase 4 (Day 6 or Later)

10$^1/_2$ tablespoons (3 oz / 85 g) whole wheat flour, whole rye flour, or unbleached bread flour

2 tablespoons (1 oz / 28.5 g) filtered or spring water

$^1/_2$ cup (4 oz / 113 g) Phase 3 seed culture

Measure out $^1/_2$ cup (4 oz / 113 g) of the Phase 3 culture and discard or give away the remainder (or save it for a second starter or as a backup). Add the new ingredients to the $^1/_2$ cup Phase 3 culture and mix to form a soft dough. Again, cover with plastic wrap and leave at room temperature until the culture becomes active. It should swell and double in size. It can take anywhere from 4 to 24 hours for the Phase 4 culture to become fully active. If there is still little sign of fermentation after 24 hours, leave it at room temperature until it becomes very active, continuing to aerate the culture at least twice daily. The seed culture should register between 3.5 and 4.0 if tested with pH paper. (Wipe a small dab on the paper and match the color against the guide.) When the culture has grown and smells acidic (somewhat like apple cider vinegar) or has a pH of 4.0 or lower, you can either proceed to the next stage or place the seed culture in the refrigerator for up to 3 days.

Second Stage: The Mother Starter

Once you've established a seed culture, you need to convert it into a mother starter. This is the starter you'll keep in your refrigerator perpetually and use to build your actual bread dough. To convert a seed culture into a mother starter, you'll use the seed culture to inoculate a larger batch of flour and water to make a firm piece of starter with the consistency of bread dough. The seed culture is full of wild yeast and bacteria, but its structure has been weakened by the buildup of acids and the ongoing activity of enzymes breaking down both protien and starch. To make the mother starter strong enough to function in a final dough, you'll build it with three times as much flour as seed culture (by weight). This 3-to-1 process will give the mother starter about the same feel as a final dough.

A little starter goes a long way, so the following instructions call for you to discard half of your seed culture or give it away. (This is great if you know another home baker who would like to avoid the work of making a seed culture.) Or if you'd prefer to keep a larger mother starter on hand, especially if you bake often or in large batches, you can convert the entire seed culture into a mother starter by doubling the weight of the new flour and water. (Some bakers like to split the seed culture into two mother starters, one wheat and one rye, but unless you are making a lot of rye bread on a regular basis, I think this is unnecessary.)

Mother Starter

$2^3/_4$ cups (12 oz / 340 g) whole wheat flour, whole rye flour, or unbleached bread flour

1 cup plus 2 tablespoons (9 oz / 255 g) filtered or spring water (or 8 oz / 227 g if using white flour)

$^3/_4$ cup (4 oz / 113 g) Phase 4 seed culture (approximately half)

Combine all of the ingredients in the bowl of an electric mixer with the paddle attachment and mix on slow speed for 1 minute. Or, combine all of the ingredients in a bowl and use a large spoon or your hands to mix until the ingredients form a rough, slightly sticky

ball. Transfer the starter to a lightly floured work surface and knead for 2 minutes, until the starter is fairly smooth and all of the ingredients are evenly distributed.

Place the mother starter in a clean, lightly oiled nonreactive bowl, crock, or plastic container large enough to contain the starter after it doubles in size. Cover loosely with plastic wrap or a lid (don't tighten the lid, as the carbon dioxide gas will need to escape). Leave the starter out at room temperature for 4 to 8 hours (or longer if needed), until it doubles in size; the timing will depend on the ambient temperature and the potency of your seed culture. Once it's doubled, the starter should register 4.0 or less if tested with pH paper and have a pleasant acidic aroma.

When the starter is fermented, degas it by kneading it for a few seconds, then form it back into a ball, cover tightly, and refrigerate. After a few hours in the refrigerator, vent any carbon dioxide buildup by briefly opening the lid or plastic wrap. The mother starter is now ready to use and will be good for up to 5 days. To use it after 5 days, you must refresh all or part of the mother starter, as described below.

Refreshing the Mother Starter

Whenever the mother starter gets low, rebuild it (also called feeding or refreshing it) using 4 ounces (113 g) of the old starter and repeating the instructions above. You can even

start with as little as 1 ounce (28.5 g) of mother starter and rebuild it in increments over a number of feedings, using the same ratios as for a 4-ounce (113 g) batch. For example, after a few weeks in the refrigerator, the protein and starches will break down, giving the starter a structure or consistency of potato soup. This is okay; the microorganisms are still viable, though fairly dormant (and maybe even a little drunk on the alcohol they've produced, which rises to the top and looks like gray water).

To rebuild your mother starter, use 1 ounce (28.5 g) of mother starter and add 3 ounces (85 g) of flour and 2 to 2.25 ounces (56.5 to 64 g) of water. This will produce about 6 ounces (170 g) of starter. You can then build all or part of that into a larger piece using the same ratios: 100 percent flour, 33.3 percent starter, and 66 to 75 percent water. So for 6 ounces (170 g) of starter, use 18 ounces (510 g) flour (6 multiplied by 3) and 12 to 13.5 ounces (340 to 383 g) water (18 multiplied by 66 percent or 75 percent—lower hydration for all white flour, higher hydration for all whole grain flour). As you see, you can build a small piece of starter into a large piece very quickly.

CHAPTER 3

French Breads and Sourdough Hearth Breads

Hearth-style breads of all types—including all of the variations on French bread and Italian bread, as well as certain types of whole grain bread—are made from lean dough. This name reflects that there are few or no enrichments, such as fats or sugars, in the dough (with exceptions here and there). Breads made from lean dough are characterized by a hard crust and a toothsome texture, so much so that in some books this category is referred to as hard dough. The hard crust is caused by the gluten protein in the flour, which hasn't been tenderized by mixing in shortening or fat.

This chapter focuses on lean dough breads based on the mixing and fermentation process in the first recipe, using a method that's similar to some of the no-knead recipes that have appeared in recent books. The dough isn't quite like traditional or classic French bread dough (that recipe is on page 49), but you'll find that the modifications in this recipe produce superior bread. This will enable you to make French-style bread of fantastic quality with very little work. For maximum ease and best results, be sure to review the specific mixing, handling, and shaping skills illustrated starting on page 16.

Lean bread (page 46), as rolls

Lean Bread

MAKES 2 LARGE LOAVES, 4 TO 6 SMALLER LOAVES, OR UP TO 24 ROLLS

Because the methods in this book balance time, temperature, and ingredients, you don't need an array of pre-ferments to accomplish full development of the flavor and texture of the bread. Time does most of the work through slow, cold overnight fermentation. This formula differs from similar approaches in other recent books by using less yeast, giving the bread better flavor and caramelization, or coloring, of the crust. The dough will keep in the refrigerator for up to a week, but after about 4 days the quality starts to decline. If you want to make a full-size batch and save some of the unbaked dough for longer than a week, place the dough in one or more lightly oiled freezer bags after the initial overnight fermentation, seal tightly, and freeze. To thaw, place the bag of dough in the refrigerator the day before you need it so that it can thaw slowly, without overfermenting. This dough also makes excellent pizza crust (see pages 67 to 73 for other variations and page 24 for shaping instructions).

$5^1/_3$ cups (24 oz / 680 g) unbleached bread flour

2 teaspoons (0.5 oz / 14 g) salt, or 1 tablespoon coarse kosher salt

2 teaspoons (0.22 oz / 6 g) instant yeast

$2^1/_4$ cups (18 oz / 510 g) lukewarm water (about 95°F or 35°C)

DO AHEAD

Combine all of the ingredients in a mixing bowl. If using a mixer, use the paddle attachment and mix on the lowest speed for 2 minutes. If mixing by hand, use a large spoon and stir for 2 minutes, until well blended. If the spoon gets too doughy, dip it in a bowl of warm water. The dough should be very soft, sticky, coarse, and shaggy, but still doughlike. Use a wet bowl scraper or spatula to transfer the dough to a clean, lightly oiled bowl. Let the dough rest for 5 minutes.

To stretch and fold the dough in the bowl, with wet or oiled hands or a wet bowl scraper, reach under the front end of the dough, stretch it out, then fold it back onto the top of the dough. Do this from the back end and then from each side, then flip the dough over and tuck it into a ball. The dough should be significantly firmer, though still very soft and fragile. Cover the bowl with plastic wrap and let the dough sit at room temperature for 10 minutes. Repeat this stretch and fold process three more times, completing all repetitions within 40 to 45 minutes. The dough will be a little firmer than when first mixed and the shaggy texture will have smoothed out somewhat, but it will still spread out to fill the bowl.

After the final stretch and fold, return the dough to the lightly oiled bowl, and immediately cover the bowl tightly and refrigerate overnight or for up to 4 days. The dough will rise to about double, and possibly triple, its original size within 4 to 12 hours in the refrigerator. (If you plan to bake the dough in batches over different days, you can portion the dough and place it into two or more oiled bowls at this stage.)

ON BAKING DAY

Remove the dough from the refrigerator about 2 hours before you plan to bake. Rub the work surface with a few drops of olive or vegetable oil, then use a wet bowl scraper or wet hands to transfer the dough to the work surface. Divide the dough in half (about 21 oz or 595 g each) for two large loaves; into 4 to 6 pieces for smaller loaves; or into 18 to 24 pieces for rolls.

Line a sheet pan with parchment paper or a silicone mat, then mist it lightly with spray oil or dust it with flour, semolina, or cornmeal. (If using a *banneton* or proofing mold, mist it with spray oil, then dust it with flour.) Have a small bowl of bread flour standing by. With floured hands, gently pat the dough pieces into rectangles, then stretch it into torpedos (see page 21), *boules* (see page 20), or loaves (see page 23), or shape it into rolls (see page 25). With floured hands, gently lift the dough and place it seam side down on the prepared pan (or seam side up in the proofing mold). If air bubbles form, pinch the surface to pop them. Mist the surface of the dough with spray oil and cover loosely with plastic wrap or a towel.

Let the shaped dough sit, covered, at room temperature for 60 minutes. Then, remove the covering and let the dough proof for an additional 60 minutes. The dough will spread slightly and the skin will begin to dry out a bit.

About 45 minutes before baking, preheat the oven to 550°F (288°C) or as high as it will go, and prepare the oven for hearth baking (see page 30).

Just before baking, score the dough with a sharp serrated knife or razor blade. The dough will have spread somewhat but should still have its basic shape, and the shape should spring back in the oven. (If using a *banneton* or proofing mold, remove the dough from the basket at this stage.) Transfer the dough to the oven, pour 1 cup of hot water into the steam pan, then lower the oven temperature to 450°F (232°C), or 425°F (218°C) for a convection oven.

Bake for 10 to 12 minutes, then rotate the pan and bake for another 10 to 15 minutes, until the crust is a rich golden brown and the internal temperature is 200°F to 205°F (93°C to 94°C). For a crisper crust, turn off the oven and leave the bread in for another 5 to 10 minutes before removing (rolls will take less time). Cool the bread on a wire rack for at least 1 hour before slicing or serving.

Classic French Bread

MAKES 2 LARGE LOAVES, 4 SMALL LOAVES, OR MANY ROLLS

This version of French bread is the simplest formula in the book. It uses the cold fermentation technique, and the resulting dough actually holds the shape and cuts of conventional French baguettes, *bâtards*, and *boules* better than the lean dough (page 46), which is wetter. Because the dough isn't as wet, it's especially important to handle it with a firm but light touch. Too much pressure will squeeze out the gas trapped during the overnight rise, resulting in small, even holes rather than the prized large, irregular holes. I've also included a variation that makes spectacular loaves with a distinctive blistered crust.

5$\frac{1}{3}$ cups (24 oz / 680 g) unbleached bread flour

2 teaspoons (0.5 oz / 14 g) salt, or 1 tablespoon coarse kosher salt

2$\frac{1}{4}$ teaspoons (0.25 oz / 7 g) instant yeast

2 cups (16 oz / 454 g) lukewarm water (about 95°F or 35°C)

DO AHEAD

Combine all of the ingredients in a mixing bowl. If using a mixer, use the paddle attachment and mix on the lowest speed for 1 minute. If mixing by hand, use a large spoon and stir for 1 minute, until well blended and smooth. If the spoon gets too doughy, dip it in a bowl of warm water. The dough should form a coarse shaggy ball. Let it rest, uncovered, for 5 minutes.

Switch to the dough hook and mix on medium-low speed for 2 minutes or knead by hand for about 2 minutes, adjusting with flour or water as needed. The dough should be smooth, supple, and tacky but not sticky.

Whichever mixing method you use, knead the dough by hand on a lightly floured work surface for about 1 minute more, then transfer it to a clean, lightly oiled bowl. Cover the bowl with plastic wrap, then immediately refrigerate overnight or for up to 4 days. If the dough feels too wet and sticky, do not add more flour; instead, stretch and fold it one or more times at 10-minute intervals, as shown on page 18, before putting it in the refrigerator. (If you plan to bake the dough in batches over different days, you can portion the dough and place it into two or more oiled bowls at this stage.)

Remove the dough from the refrigerator about 2 hours before you plan to bake. Gently transfer it to a lightly floured work surface, taking care to degas it as little as possible. For baguettes and *bâtards*, divide the cold dough into 10-ounce (283 g) pieces; for 1 pound *boules*, divide the dough into 19-ounce (53 g) pieces; and for freestanding loaves, use whatever size you prefer.

Form the dough into *bâtards* and/or baguettes (see pages 21 and 22) or *boules* (see page 20). Mist the top of the dough with spray oil, loosely cover with plastic wrap, and proof at room temperature for about $1^1/_2$ hours, until increased to $1^1/_2$ times its original size.

About 45 minutes before baking, preheat the oven to 550°F (288°C) or as high as it will go, and prepare the oven for hearth baking (see page 30).

Remove the plastic wrap from the dough 15 minutes prior to baking; if using proofing molds, transfer the dough onto a floured peel.

Just prior to baking, score the dough $^1/_2$ inch deep with a serrated knife or razor. Transfer the dough to the oven, pour 1 cup of hot water into the steam pan, then lower the oven temperature to 450°F (232°C).

Bake for 12 minutes, then rotate the pan and bake for another 15 to 25 minutes, until the crust is a rich golden brown, the loaves sound hollow when thumped, and the internal temperature is about 200°F (93°C) in the center. For a crisper crust, turn off the oven and leave the bread in for another 5 minutes before removing.

Cool the bread on a wire rack for at least 45 minutes before slicing or serving.

VARIATION

By simply varying the method so that the shaped loaves undergo cold fermentation, rather than the freshly mixed bulk dough, you can create a spectacular loaf with a distinctive blistered crust. After the dough is mixed and placed in a clean, oiled bowl, let it rise at room temperature for about 90 minutes, until doubled in size. Divide and shape as described above, mist with spray oil, then cover the shaped dough loosely with plastic wrap and refrigerate it overnight, away from anything that might fall on it or restrict it from growing.

The next day, remove the dough from the refrigerator 1 hour before baking. It should have grown to at least $1^1/_2$ times its original size. Prepare the oven for hearth baking, as described on page 30. While the oven is heating, remove the plastic wrap and let the dough sit uncovered for 10 minutes. Score the dough while it's still cold, then bake as described above.

Pain à l'Ancienne Rustic Bread

MAKES 2 LARGE CIABATTA LOAVES, 3 SMALL
CIABATTA LOAVES, OR 6 TO 8 MINI BAGUETTES

I first introduced the concept of cold-fermented wet dough in *The Bread Baker's Apprentice*. While the idea isn't new or original, it has blossomed during the past few years into various no-knead, overnight-rise permutations. I now prefer the version in this recipe because it gives the best flavor and also provides the most flexibility for scheduling. The refrigerator provides a 4-day window of baking opportunity, and that's hard to beat. The beauty of this dough, as others have discovered, is that it can be used in so many ways: for focaccia, ciabatta, mini baguettes, and more. (Because the method for shaping this dough into focaccia is substantially different, it appears as a separate recipe on page 57.) And even though it's the most hydrated dough in this book, it requires only minimal mixing to achieve the same gluten strength as bakeries obtain by mixing continuously for 20 minutes, due to the stretch and fold technique.

4$^{1}/_{2}$ cups (20 oz / 567 g) unbleached bread flour
1$^{3}/_{4}$ teaspoons (0.4 oz / 11 g) salt, or 2$^{1}/_{2}$ teaspoons coarse kosher salt
1$^{1}/_{4}$ teaspoons (0.14 oz / 4 g) instant yeast
2 cups (16 oz / 454 g) chilled water (about 55°F or 13°C)
1 tablespoon (0.5 oz / 14 g) olive oil (for ciabatta only)

DO AHEAD

Combine the flour, salt, yeast, and water in a mixing bowl. If using a mixer, use the paddle attachment and mix on the lowest speed for 1 minute. If mixing by hand, use a large spoon and stir for about 1 minute, until well blended. The dough should be coarse and sticky. Let the dough rest for 5 minutes to fully hydrate the flour.

If making ciabatta, drizzle the olive oil over the dough; if making mini baguettes, omit the oil. Then mix on medium-low speed using the paddle attachment, or by hand using a large, wet spoon or wet hands, for 1 minute. The dough should become smoother but will still be very soft, sticky, and wet. Use a wet bowl scraper or spatula to transfer the dough to a clean, lightly oiled bowl. Cover the bowl with plastic wrap and let the dough rest at room temperature for 10 minutes.

Transfer the dough to a lightly oiled work surface. With wet or oiled hands, reach under the front end of the dough, stretch it out, then fold it back onto the top of the dough. Do this

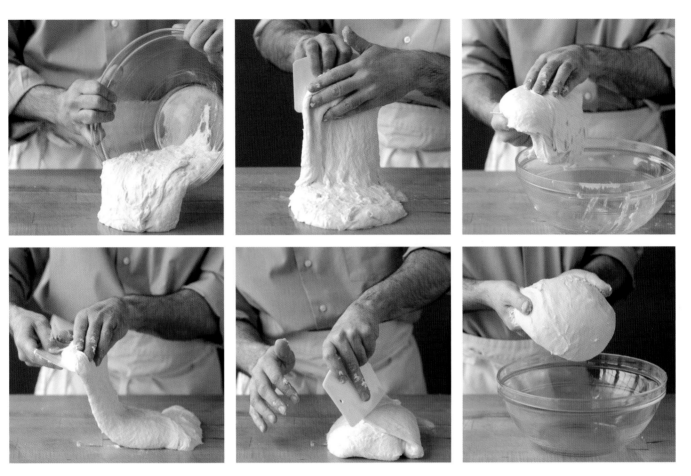

To stretch and fold the dough on the work surface, lightly oil the surface and your hands, then transfer the dough to the surface. Stretch one end of the dough out then fold it back over the top of the dough. Do this from all four sides then place the dough back in the bowl and let sit for 10 minutes. Repeat this process three more times. You will feel the dough become significantly firmer.

from the back end and then from each side, then flip the dough over and tuck it into a ball. The dough should be significantly firmer, though still very soft and fragile. Place the dough back in the bowl, cover, and let sit at room temperature for 10 minutes. Repeat this process three more times, completing all repetitions within 40 minutes. (You can also perform the stretch and folds in the bowl, as shown on page 17.)

After the final stretch and fold, immediately cover the bowl tightly and refrigerate overnight or for up to 4 days. The dough will rise, possibly to double its original size, in the refrigerator. (If you plan to bake the dough in batches over different days, you can portion the dough and place it into two or more oiled bowls at this stage.)

ON BAKING DAY

Remove the dough from the refrigerator about 1 hour before baking for mini baguettes, and 3 hours in advance for ciabatta (or an hour earlier if the dough hasn't increased to $1^1/_2$ times its original size in the refrigerator overnight).

To make ciabatta, about 1 hour after taking the dough out of the refrigerator, line the back of a sheet pan with parchment paper and generously dust the entire surface with flour. Use a wet or oiled bowl scraper to transfer the dough to the work surface, taking care to handle the dough as little as possible to avoid degassing it.

Dust the top surface of the dough with flour and also flour your hands. Using your hands or a metal pastry scraper, gently coax and pat the dough into a rough square measuring about 9 inches on each side, still taking care to degas it as little as possible.

For small ciabatta, cut the dough into 3 even strips about 3 inches wide and 9 inches long (the pieces will each weigh about 12 ounces or 340 grams). For larger ciabatta, cut the dough in half. With floured hands, gently fold the dough in thirds, like folding a letter but without applying any pressure. Gently roll the folded dough in the dusting flour to coat it, then lift the dough and place it on the parchment paper, again rolling it in the dusting flour

on the parchment. Rest the dough seam side down on the parchment and repeat with the other pieces of dough.

Mist the tops of the dough pieces with spray oil and loosely cover the pan with plastic wrap or a clean, lint-free towel. After 1 hour, gently roll the pieces over so the seam side is up, lift and cradle each piece with floured hands, and, working from the underside, gently coax it to a length of 5 inches (for small ciabatta) to 7 inches (for large ciabatta). Lay the pieces back on the parchment seam side up. Straighten the sides of each piece with your hands or a pastry scraper so that they are more rectangular than oblong, mist with spray oil again, then cover loosely and proof for 1 hour more.

About 45 minutes before baking, preheat the oven to 550°F (288°C) or as high as it will go, and prepare the oven for hearth baking (see page 30).

Slide the dough, parchment and all, onto the stone; if you aren't using a baking stone, simply put the whole pan into the oven. Pour 1 cup of hot water into the steam pan, then lower the oven temperature to 450°F (232°C).

Bake for 12 minutes, then rotate the pan and bake for 15 to 20 minutes more, until the crust is a rich brown (streaked with the dusting flour). The bread should puff a little, and the crust should be hard when tapped (it'll soften as it cools). Cool on a wire rack for 45 minutes before slicing.

To make mini baguettes, about 45 minutes before baking, preheat the oven to 550°F (288°C), or as high as it will go, and prepare the oven for hearth baking (see page 30). After the dough has been out for 1 hour, generously dust the entire surface of a wooden peel with flour or line the back of a sheet pan with parchment paper (you can either dust the parchment with flour or mist it with spray oil so that you can slide and move the dough if need be). Use a wet or oiled bowl scraper to transfer the dough from the bowl to the work surface, taking care to handle the dough as little as possible to avoid degassing it.

Dust the top surface of the dough with flour and also flour your hands. Using your hands or a metal pastry scraper, gently coax and pat the dough into a rough square about 8 inches on each side, still taking care to degas it as little as possible.

Cut off a slice of dough about $1^1/_2$ inches wide and roll it into the dusting flour to lightly coat it and keep it from sticking to the remainder of the dough. Working with floured hands

and tools, carefully transfer the slice to the prepared peel or parchment paper, cradling it with both hands to keep it from stretching too much. You can straighten it by spreading your hands underneath the dough as you lay it down; it should elongate slightly, to 9 to 10 inches.

Repeat with the rest of the dough, placing the pieces 1 inch apart, until the peel or parchment is full. If you can't fit all of the pieces on the peel or parchment, bake those that are ready before cutting the remainder. It's better to work in manageable batches than to try to cram all of them in the oven, especially if your stone or oven won't easily hold all of them. Scoring the dough is an option, but because it risks degassing the dough, I advise against it until you have made these a few times.

Slide the mini baguettes onto the baking stone using short, quick back-and-forth motions with the peel, or by sliding the parchment paper onto the stone. Pour $^1/_2$ cup of hot water into the steam pan, then lower the oven temperature to 475°F (246°C).

Bake for 12 to 18 minutes total, rotating the pan as needed for even browning. The crust should be a rich brown, the loaves should puff a little, and the crust should be hard when tapped (the crust will soften slightly as the bread cools).

Cool on a wire rack for at least 15 minutes.

VARIATION

For an interesting ciabatta texture and a nice design on the surface of the bread, mix a small amount of coarse rye flour or whole wheat flour in with the dusting flour.

Pain à l'Ancienne Focaccia

Although this formula is exactly the same as the preceeding *pain à l'ancienne* rustic bread recipe (page 52), the method is quite different. This focaccia dough is also quite similar to the pizza doughs in this book, the main difference being the amount of hydration. Focaccia is wetter, at 80 percent hydration, because it has the benefit of rising and baking in a pan to provide structural support, whereas pizza dough is closer to 70 percent hydration so that it can be handled and stretched. In both cases, the dough should be slightly sticky, not just tacky. Focaccia dough is so wet that it's best to use olive oil to handle it, whereas flour works just fine with pizza dough. You can also bake a smaller, round focaccia (pictured on page 198).

$4^1/_2$ cups (20 oz / 567 g) unbleached bread flour

$1^3/_4$ teaspoons (0.4 oz / 11 g) salt, or $2^1/_2$ teaspoons coarse kosher salt

$1^1/_4$ teaspoons (0.14 oz / 4 g) instant yeast

2 cups (16 oz / 454 g) chilled water (about 55°F or 13°C)

1 tablespoon (0.5 oz / 14 g) olive oil, plus more for the pan

DO AHEAD

Combine the flour, salt, yeast, and water in a mixing bowl. If using a mixer, use the paddle attachment and mix on the lowest speed for 1 minute. If mixing by hand, use a large spoon and stir for about 1 minute, until well blended. The dough should be coarse and wet. Let the dough rest for 5 minutes to fully hydrate the flour.

Drizzle the olive oil over the dough, then resume mixing on medium-low speed using the paddle attachment, or by hand using a large wet spoon or wet hands, for 1 minute. The dough should become smoother but will still be very soft, sticky, and wet. Use a wet bowl scraper or spatula to transfer the dough to a clean, lightly oiled bowl. Cover the bowl with plastic wrap and let the dough rest at room temperature for 10 minutes.

Transfer the dough to a lightly oiled work surface. With wet or oiled hands, reach under the front end of the dough, stretch it out, then fold it back onto the top of the dough. Do this from the back end and then from each side, then flip the dough over and tuck it into a ball. The dough should be significantly firmer, though still very soft and fragile. Place the dough back in the bowl, cover, and let sit at room temperature for 10 minutes. Repeat this entire process three more times, completing all repetitions within 30 to 40 minutes. (You can also do the stretch and folds in the bowl, as shown on page 17.)

After the final stretch and fold, return the dough to the oiled bowl and immediately cover the bowl tightly and refrigerate overnight or for up to 4 days, or pan it immediately (as described below).

To make 1 large focaccia, line a 12 by 16-inch sheet pan with parchment paper or a silicone mat. Oil it generously, including the sides, with about 2 tablespoons of olive oil, then transfer the dough to the pan. Drizzle another tablespoon of oil over the top of the dough, then use your fingertips to dimple the dough and spread it to cover about half of the pan. Make sure the top of the dough is coated with oil, then cover the pan (not the dough) tightly with plastic wrap and immediately place the pan in the refrigerator overnight or for up to 4 days.

For round focaccia, cut out a piece of parchment paper to fit inside an 8- or 9-inch round pan. Oil both the parchment and the sides of the pan with 1 tablespoon of olive oil, then transfer the dough to the pan. For an 8-inch pan, use 8 ounces (227 g) of dough; for a 9-inch pan, use 12 ounces (340 g) of dough. Drizzle 1 teaspoon of olive oil over the top of the dough, then use your fingertips to dimple the dough and spread it as far as it will allow. Don't force the dough when it starts to spring back. Cover the pan (not the dough) tightly with plastic wrap and immediately place the pan in the refrigerator overnight or for up to 4 days.

ON BAKING DAY

Remove the dough from the refrigerator about $2^{1}/_{2}$ hours before you plan to bake, and if you haven't already panned it, follow the instructions above to do so, spreading it to cover a portion of the pan.

Warm the oven for just a few minutes, then turn it off; or, if you have a gas oven with a pilot light, it's warm enough without any heating. Drizzle a small amount of olive oil on the surface of the dough and, beginning in the center and working toward the sides, dimple the dough

One possible topping for focaccia is herb oil (page 70); you can add it during the final dimpling.

with your fingertips to spread it over more of the pan. The dough will start resisting and sliding back toward the center after a minute of this; stop dimpling at that point. It should now be covering 70 to 80 percent of the pan. Cover the pan with plastic wrap and put it in the warm oven (with the heat off!). For a gas oven with a pilot light, leave the focaccia in for just 5 minutes. Otherwise, leave it in for about 8 minutes. (If you have plenty of time, you can simply let the dough rest at room temperature for 30 minutes between dimplings, which will require a total of about 4 hours prior to baking.)

After the focaccia has been out of the oven for 10 minutes, remove the plastic wrap, drizzle another small amount of olive oil over the dough, and dimple it again. This time it should cover about 90 percent of the pan. Cover it again and return it to the warm oven for 5 minutes in a gas oven with a pilot light or 10 to 20 minutes for any other type of oven. On the third dimpling (if not the second), the dough should evenly fill the entire pan. If it creeps in from the corners because of the oil, don't worry; it will fill the corners as it rises. Cover the pan with plastic wrap and proof the dough in the slightly warm oven as before, removing it after 5 to 10 minutes and completing the rise at room temperature. It should be about 1 inch high in 1 to $1^{1}/_{2}$ hours (longer if not using the oven).

Preheat the oven to 500°F (260°C). (You don't need a baking stone, but if you'd like to use one, allow 45 minutes for it to preheat.) Top the focaccia with your choice of toppings (see page 70 for topping ideas), but wait until the end of the baking time to add any cheese.

Place the pan in the oven. **For large focaccia,** lower the oven temperature to 450°F (232°C) and bake for 12 minutes. Rotate the pan and bake for another 10 to 15 minutes, until the top of the dough is golden brown. **For round focaccia,** keep the oven temperature at 500°F (260°C) and bake for 10 to 12 minutes. If you use moist toppings, such as fresh tomatoes or sauce, the focaccia will take longer to bake. To test for doneness, use a metal spatula to lift the edge of the focaccia so you can see the underside; it should be a mottled golden brown in spots, not white all over. If you're topping the focaccia with cheese, add it when the focaccia appears to be done, then bake for another 2 to 4 minutes to melt the cheese.

When you remove the focaccia from the oven, run a pastry blade or metal spatula along the sides of the pan to loosen the focaccia, then carefully slide the focaccia, parchment and all, onto a wire rack. If any olive oil remains in the pan, pour it over the top of the focaccia. Cool for at least 10 minutes before serving.

Pain au Levain

MAKES 1 LARGE LOAF OR 2 SMALL LOAVES

Pain au levain, which is the French term for naturally leavened bread, is generally considered to be the gold standard for wild yeast breads, though opinions do vary widely—and are strongly held. People from San Francisco, Portland, New York, Boston, anywhere in Germany (where it is called *Sauerteig*), and many other cities and regions may dispute the superiority of the French version. In fact, there isn't one single version of *pain au levain*; it's really a category of bread, usually consisting primarily of white flour, supplemented with a small amount of whole wheat flour, rye flour, or a multigrain flour. To complicate matters further, some "authentic" French *levains* are made with all-natural starter, while others use a combination of starter and commercial yeast (usually just a small amount). In this book, I use the term *pain au levain* to indicate breads that are naturally leavened, either with or without the addition of commercial yeast, using anywhere from 5 to 20 percent whole grain flour.

In the process of developing the formulas for *Peter Reinhart's Whole Grain Breads*, I discovered a method of mixing natural starters with commercial yeast that seems to work especially well for home baking and small batches. By increasing the amount of starter and commercial yeast in the final dough, it's possible to make breads with all of the flavor development of the great *levains*, but with a shortened proofing stage at the end. As with most of the breads in this book, the cold, overnight fermentation method also extends the life of the dough to at least 3 days, with flavors that are even more developed on the third day than on the first. Although this unconventional recipe is unlike anything you'll find in other books, it follows and fulfills the flavor rule (that is, flavor rules!).

As with the San Francisco sourdough (page 64), you can make this bread leavened only with natural starter (the "purist" method), or you can add instant yeast to the final dough (the mixed method). If you want to use the "purist" method and bake the bread on the same day as you mix the dough, don't refrigerate the final dough; just let it rest at room temperature for about 4 hours, or until it doubles in size. Then, shape and proof it at room temperature for about $1^1/_2$ to 2 hours, and bake as described below.

SOURDOUGH STARTER

$^1/_3$ cup (2.5 oz / 71 g) mother starter (page 42), cold or at room temperature

1 cup plus 2 tablespoons (5 oz / 142 g) unbleached bread flour

$^2/_3$ cup (3 oz / 85 g) whole wheat flour

$^2/_3$ cup (5.35 oz / 151.5 g) water, at room temperature

continued

All of the sourdough starter (16 oz / 458 g)

1 cup plus 6 tablespoons (11 oz / 312 g) lukewarm water
(about 95°F or 35°C)

2¹/₄ teaspoons (0.25 oz / 7 g) instant yeast (optional)

3¹/₂ cups (16 oz / 454 g) unbleached bread flour

2³/₈ teaspoons (0.6 oz / 17 g) salt, or 3¹/₂ teaspoons coarse kosher salt

DO AHEAD

To make the starter, combine all of the ingredients in a mixing bowl. If using a mixer, use the paddle attachment and mix on the lowest speed for 1 minute, then increase to medium speed for about 30 seconds. If mixing by hand, use a large spoon and stir for about 2 minutes, until well blended. The starter should feel doughlike and tacky or slightly sticky; if not, stir in additional flour or water as needed.

Transfer the starter to a lightly floured work surface and knead for about 30 seconds. Place it in a clean, lightly oiled bowl, cover the bowl loosely, and leave at room temperature for 6 to 8 hours, until the starter increases to about 1¹/₂ times its original size. If you plan to use the starter the same day, allow 1 more hour of fermentation so that it nearly doubles in size. Otherwise, put the starter in the refrigerator for up to 3 days.

To make the dough, cut the starter into 10 to 12 pieces and put them in a mixing bowl. Pour in the water, then add the yeast (unless you're making the "purist" version) and mix with the paddle attachment on the lowest speed or by hand with a large spoon for about 1 minute to soften the starter. Add the flour and salt.

Switch to the dough hook and mix on the lowest speed, or continue mixing by hand, for 3 minutes, to form a coarse ball of dough that's very tacky and slightly warm. Let the dough rest for 5 minutes.

Resume mixing on medium-low speed for 3 minutes more or knead by hand for 3 minutes, adding more flour or water as needed to make a soft, supple, and tacky but not sticky ball of dough.

Knead the dough by hand for a few seconds, then form it into a ball. Let the dough sit uncovered for 10 minutes, then do a stretch and fold, either on the work surface or in the bowl, reaching under the front end of the dough, stretching it out, then folding it back onto the top of the dough. Do this from the back end and then from each side, then flip the dough over and tuck it into a ball. Cover the dough and let it rest for 10 minutes. Repeat this entire process two more times, completing all repetitions within 30 minutes. Immediately form the dough into a ball, place it in a clean, lightly oiled bowl large enough to contain the dough when it doubles in size, and cover the bowl tightly.

If using the mixed method with instant yeast, refrigerate the dough immediately. If making the "purist" version, without instant yeast, let the dough sit at room temperature for 2 hours before refrigerating; it won't rise very much, but it should show signs of growth and continue to rise in the refrigerator. Either version will be ready to use the next day and for up to 4 days. (If you plan to bake the dough in batches over different days, you can portion the dough and place it into two or more oiled bowls at this stage.)

ON BAKING DAY

For the "purist" version, remove the dough from the refrigerator about 4 hours before you plan to bake; after 2 hours, shape it (see instructions for lean bread, page 48), then let it proof for 2 hours before baking. For the mixed method, remove the dough from the refrigerator 2 hours prior to baking and shape it right away. Remove only the portion you wish to bake: 19 ounces (539 g) for a 1-pound (454 g) loaf; 28 ounces (794 g) for a 1¹/₂-pound (680 g) loaf, and so on. You can also bake the entire amount of dough as a large, 3-pound (1.36 kg) *miche* (round country loaf) or as a large torpedo loaf. Gently transfer it from the bowl to a lightly floured work surface, being careful to degas it as little as possible. See chapter 1, starting on page 20, for shaping and proofing instructions. The shaped dough won't increase in size very much, but it will begin to swell and grow. If it grows to 1¹/₂ times its original size in less than 2 hours, move on to the scoring and baking stage.

If using a baking stone, about 45 minutes before baking preheat the oven to 500°F (260°C) and prepare the oven for hearth baking (see page 30). Otherwise, just preheat the oven to 500°F (260°C) about 20 minutes before baking.

Just before baking, score the dough in whatever style of design you prefer, as shown on page 29. Transfer the dough to the oven, pour 1 cup of hot water into the steam pan, then lower the oven temperature to 450°F (232°C), or to 425°F (218°C) if baking a large *miche*.

Bake for 12 minutes, then rotate the pan and continue baking for 15 to 25 minutes, or longer, depending on the size of the loaf; a large *miche* could take up to 75 minutes to bake. When fully baked, the crust should have a rich, caramelized color; the loaf should sound hollow when thumped on the bottom; and the internal temperature should be about 200°F (90°C) in the center.

Cool on a wire rack for at least 1 hour before slicing or serving.

San Francisco Sourdough Bread

I've developed two ways to make San Francisco–style sourdough bread using the overnight method. The "purist" method of making sourdough breads uses no commercial yeast and produces a flavor that's tart, acidic, and complex. The mixed method uses instant yeast to produce a finished loaf more quickly; because of the reduced fermentation time, it yields less acidity and sourness. Both versions are excellent. To use the wild yeast starter, build and ripen your starter at least 1 day and not more than 3 days prior to making the final dough.

Of course, if you don't live in San Francisco, this won't be true San Francisco sourdough bread because it won't contain a large concentration of the microorganisms associated with the Bay Area, especially the famous *Lactobacillus sanfranciscensis* (these organisms do exist in sourdoughs everywhere, but not to the same extent as they do in and around San Francisco). However, this style of sourdough, made with all unbleached white bread flour, has become so closely associated with San Francisco that I call it San Francisco sourdough to distinguish it from the French *pain au levain*, which contains a small amount of whole grain flour. That said, any number of *pain au levain* variations can be made by simply substituting whole grain or other flours for some of the white flour.

WILD YEAST STARTER

1/4 cup (2 oz / 56.5 g) mother starter, cold or at room temperature

1³/4 cups (8 oz / 227 g) unbleached bread flour

1/2 cup plus 2 tablespoons (5 oz / 142 g) water, at room temperature

DOUGH

All of the wild yeast starter (15 oz / 425 g)

1³/4 cups (14 oz / 397 g) lukewarm water (about 95°F or 35°C)

4¹/2 cups (20 oz / 567 g) unbleached bread flour

2¹/2 teaspoons (0.63 oz / 18 g) salt, or 3¹/2 teaspoons coarse kosher salt

2¹/4 teaspoons (0.25 oz / 7 g) instant yeast (optional)

To make the starter, combine all of the ingredients in a mixing bowl. If using a mixer, use the paddle attachment and mix on the lowest speed for 1 minute, then increase to medium speed for about 30 seconds. If mixing by hand, stir for about 2 minutes, until well blended. The starter should feel doughlike and tacky or slightly sticky; if not, stir in additional flour or water as needed.

Transfer the starter to a lightly floured work surface and knead for about 30 seconds. Place it in a clean, lightly oiled bowl, cover the bowl loosely, and leave at room temperature for 6 to 8 hours, until the starter increases to about $1^1/_2$ times its original size. If you plan to use the starter the same day, allow 1 more hour of fermentation so that it nearly doubles in size. Otherwise, put the starter in the refrigerator for up to 3 days.

To make the dough, cut the starter into 10 to 12 pieces and put them in a mixing bowl. Pour in the water and mix with the paddle attachment on the lowest speed or with a large spoon for about 1 minute to soften the starter.

Add the flour and salt, as well as the yeast (unless you're making the "purist" version). Switch to the dough hook and mix on the lowest speed, or continue mixing by hand, for 2 minutes, to form a coarse ball of dough that's very tacky and slightly warm. Let the dough rest for 5 minutes.

Mix on medium-low speed or by hand for 4 minutes more, adding flour or water as needed to make a soft, supple, slightly sticky ball of dough.

Transfer the dough to a lightly floured work surface and knead by hand for 1 minute, then form it into a ball. Let the dough sit uncovered for 10 minutes, then do a stretch and fold, either on the work surface or in the bowl, reaching under the front end of the dough, stretching it out, then folding it back onto the top of the dough. Do this from the back end and then from each side, then flip the dough over and tuck it into a ball. Cover the dough and let it rest for 10 minutes. Do another stretch and fold, then immediately form the dough into a ball, place it in a clean, lightly oiled bowl large enough to contain the dough when it doubles in size, and cover the bowl.

If using the mixed method with instant yeast, refrigerate the dough immediately. If making the "purist" version, without instant yeast, let the dough sit at room temperature for $1^1/_2$ to 2 hours before refrigerating; it won't rise very much, but it should show signs of growth and continue to rise in the refrigerator. Either version will be ready to use the next day and for up to 3 days. (If you plan to bake the dough in batches over different days, you can portion the dough and place it into two or more oiled bowls at this stage.)

For the "purist" version, remove the dough from the refrigerator about 4 hours before you plan to bake; after 2 hours, shape it (see instructions for lean bread, page 48), then let it proof for 2 hours before baking. For the mixed method, remove the dough from the refrigerator 2 hours prior to baking and shape it right away. Remove only the portion you wish to bake: 19 ounces (539 g) for a 1-pound (454 g) loaf; 28 ounces (794 g) for a 1¹/₂-pound (680 g) loaf, and so on. You can also bake the entire amount of dough as a large, 3-pound (1.36 kg) *miche* (round country loaf) or as a large torpedo loaf. See chapter 1, page 20, for instructions.

Proof for 2 hours as a freestanding loaf, in floured proofing baskets, or on proofing cloths. The dough should increase in size to 1¹/₂ times its original size and be springy yet hold an indentation when pressed with a finger. It may spread as it rises, but it will grow taller as it bakes.

If using a baking stone, about 45 minutes before baking preheat the oven to 500°F (260°C) and prepare the oven for hearth baking (see page 30). Otherwise, just preheat the oven to 500°F (260°C) about 20 minutes before baking.

Just before baking, score the dough with whatever style of design you prefer (see page 29). Transfer the dough to the oven, pour 1 cup of hot water into the steam pan, then lower the oven temperature to 450°F (232°C), or to 425°F (218°C) if baking a large *miche*.

Bake for 12 minutes, then rotate the pan and continue baking for 15 to 35 minutes, or longer, depending on the size of the loaf; a large *miche* could take up to 75 minutes to bake. When fully baked, the crust should have a rich, caramelized color, the loaf should sound hollow when thumped on the bottom, and the internal temperature should be about 200°F (90°C) in the center. Cool on a wire rack for at least 1 hour before slicing or serving.

VARIATIONS

For country-style *pain au levain*, you can substitute whole wheat flour or other whole grain flours for an equal amount of bread flour (by weight), in which case you'll need to increase the water by about ¹/₂ tablespoon (0.25 oz / 7 g) for every 3¹/₂ tablespoons (1 oz / 28.5 g) of whole grain flour you use. A typical *pain au levain* would substitute 2 to 3 ounces (56.5 to 85 g) of whole grain flour for an equal amount of bread flour, but there really is no limit.

One of the best variations of this bread has crumbled blue cheese (or chunks of any good melting cheese) and toasted nuts or seeds (walnuts are highly recommended). Add nuts to the dough during the last minute of mixing, using about 25 percent nuts to total flour. Since the total flour in this recipe is about 34 ounces (964 g), counting the flour in the starter, about 8.5 ounces (241 g) of nuts would be just right. With the cheese, you can add anywhere between 25 to 45 percent of the weight of the flour; so that would be 8.5 to 15.3 ounces (241 to 434 g). Fold the cheese in by hand at the end of the mixing or roll it into the dough during shaping (see the crusty cheese bread recipe on page 121).

Neo-Neopolitan Pizza Dough

Pizzerias have long known the value of overnight, delayed fermentation, and I've written about this extensively in *American Pie: My Search for the Perfect Pizza*, as well as in other books. After teaching hundreds of pizza and focaccia classes around the country and assessing the relative benefits of the many versions of pizza dough that I wrote about in other books, I'm including and updating the most popular versions here.

This recipe is a variation of the neo-Neapolitan dough I introduced in *Amercian Pie*. I recommend making individual size pizzas, because the heat in home ovens simply isn't sufficient to do a good job on larger pizzas. This dough will keep for up to 4 days in the refrigerator or for months in the freezer; just be sure to move it from the freezer to the refrigerator the day before you need it, so it can thaw slowly, then treat it like refrigerated dough. Both the sugar and the oil in this formula are optional. If you leave them out, you have a Napoletana dough (though not a true pizza Napoletana dough unless you use Italian "00" flour, which is softer and more extensible than American flour and does not require as much water). However, in my pizza classes across the country, this version, which is similar to the dough used at some of the top American pizzerias (such as Frank Pepe's, Sally's, Totonno's, and Lombardi's), always gets the most votes for favorite.

$5^{1}/_{3}$ cups (24 oz / 680 g) unbleached bread flour

2 teaspoons (0.5 oz / 14 g) salt, or 1 tablespoon coarse kosher salt

1 teaspoon (0.11 oz / 3 g) instant yeast

2 tablespoons (1 oz / 28.5 g) sugar, or $1^{1}/_{2}$ tablespoons honey
or agave nectar (optional)

2 cups plus 2 tablespoons (17 oz / 482 g) water, at room temperature

2 tablespoons (1 oz / 28.5 g) olive oil (optional)

DO AHEAD

Combine all of the ingredients in a mixing bowl. If using a mixer, use the paddle attachment and mix on the lowest speed for 1 minute. If mixing by hand, use a large spoon and stir for about 1 minute, until well blended. The dough should be coarse and slightly sticky. Let the dough rest for 5 minutes to fully hydrate the flour.

continued

Switch to the dough hook and mix on medium-low speed, or continue mixing by hand, for 2 to 3 minutes, until the dough is smoother but still soft, supple, and somewhere between tacky and sticky.

Spread 1 teaspoon of olive oil on a work surface, then use a bowl scraper to transfer the dough to the oiled surface. Rub your hands with the oil on the work surface, then stretch and fold the dough one time, reaching under the front end of the dough, stretching it out, then folding it back onto the top of the dough. Do this from the back end and then from each side, then flip the dough over and tuck it into a ball. Divide the dough into 5 equal pieces, each weighing about 8 ounces (227 g). Form each piece into a ball, then place each into a separate sandwich-size freezer bag misted with spray oil. (Or, if you have room in the refrigerator, you can form the dough into tight balls and refrigerate them on a pan, as described below.) Seal the bag and refrigerate overnight or for up to 4 days, or in the freezer for several months.

ON BAKING DAY

About 90 minutes before you plan to bake the pizzas, place the desired number of dough balls on a lightly oiled work surface. With oiled hands, stretch and round each piece into a tight ball, then place them on a pan that's been lightly oiled (preferably with olive oil). Loosely cover with plastic wrap and let rest at room temperature until ready to bake.

About 1 hour before baking the pizzas, preheat the oven and a baking stone as high as the oven will go. If you don't have a pizza stone, you can assemble the pizzas on baking sheets covered with parchment paper and bake them on the pans. While the oven is preheating, prepare your cheeses, sauce, and toppings (see page 70).

When ready to assemble and bake, put about 1 cup (4.5 oz / 128 g) of flour in a bowl. Use some of it to dust the work surface, your hands, and the peel, if you have one. Put one of the pizza dough balls in the flour to coat the bottom. Transfer to the work surface and gently tap it down with your fingers to form a disk. Slide the backs of your hands under the dough, then lift it and begin to rotate it, using your thumbs to coax the edges of the dough into a larger circle (see page 25 for photos of this process). Don't stretch the dough with the backs of your hands or your knuckles, let your thumbs do all of the work; your hands and knuckles merely provide a platform to support the dough. If the dough starts to resist and shrink back, set it on the floured work surface and let it rest for a minute or two. You can move on to another dough ball, repeating the same gentle stretching. Continue working the dough and resting it as need be until it is about 10 to 12 inches in diameter. It should be thicker at the edges than in the center and the center should be thin but not paper-thin. If the dough rips, you can try to patch it, or you can form it back into a ball, move on to another dough ball, and try again in 15 to 20 minutes.

When the crust is ready to be topped, place it on the floured peel. Use flour rather than cornmeal or semolina, as it doesn't burn as quickly in the oven. Top the pizza as desired, then slide it onto the baking stone. If you aren't using a baking stone, just put the panned pizza in the oven.

Bake for about 4 minutes, then use the peel or a spatula to rotate the pizza. It will take anywhere from 5 to 7 minutes for the pizza to fully bake, depending on the oven (convection ovens bake faster). The edge should puff up and be a deep golden brown, perhaps even slightly charred.

Remove the pizza, garnish as desired, then let it cool for 1 minute before slicing or serving.

Sourdough Pizza Dough

MAKES 5 INDIVIDUAL PIZZAS

This recipe uses sourdough starter primarily as a flavor enhancer rather than for leavening. It adds a subtle complexity without drawing attention to itself. However, if you prefer a more tart flavor you can omit the instant yeast and give the dough four hours of fermentation at room temperature before dividing it into dough balls and refrigerating.

SOURDOUGH STARTER

2 tablespoons (1 oz / 28.5 g) mother starter (page 42), cold or at room temperature

6 tablespoons (3 oz / 85 g) water, at room temperature

3/4 cup plus 2 tablespoons (4 oz / 113 g) unbleached bread flour

DOUGH

All of the sourdough starter (8 oz / 226 g), cold or at room temperature

1 1/2 cups (12 oz / 340 g) lukewarm water (about 95°F or 35°C)

4 cups (18 oz / 510 g) unbleached bread flour

2 teaspoons (0.5 oz / 14 g) salt, or 1 tablespoon coarse kosher salt

1 teaspoon (0.11 oz / 3 g) instant yeast

2 tablespoons (1 oz / 28.5 g) sugar, or 1 1/2 tablespoons honey or agave nectar

2 tablespoons (1 oz / 28.5 g) olive oil

To make the starter, combine all of the ingredients and stir to distribute the mother starter evenly; it should have the consistency of wet dough. Place the starter in a clean, lightly oiled bowl, cover the bowl with plastic wrap, and let it ferment for 6 to 8 hours at room temperature. It will swell considerably and nearly double in size. It can be used immediately or held for up to 4 days in the refrigerator.

To make the pizza dough, cut the starter into about 12 pieces. Pour the lukewarm water into a mixing bowl, add the starter, and use your hands to break up the starter and incorporate it with the water.

Pizza and Focaccia Toppings

Remember that pizza or focaccia is simply dough with something on it, so feel free to experiment with flavorful toppings. Because focaccia is thicker than pizza it often takes longer to bake, so some toppings are better left off until the final few minutes of baking, especially dry cheeses such as parmesan (focaccia baked in round cake pans perform more like pizzas, so they can be fully topped prior to going into the oven). Some ingredients, like fresh pesto or aioli, are even better when added after the pizza or focaccia has finished baking.

Most commercial pizza sauces work fine, but if you enjoy making your own, which is quite easy and highly recommended, remember that canned tomato products do not need to be heated up or cooked since they will be cooked on the pizza or focaccia. Here are my favorite sauce and herb oil recipes.

CRUSHED TOMATO SAUCE	MAKES 4 CUPS
1 can (28 oz / 794 g) crushed tomatoes	
1/4 teaspoon freshly ground black pepper	
1 teaspoon dried basil or 2 tablespoons minced fresh basil (optional)	
1 teaspoon dried oregano or 1 tablespoon minced fresh oregano (optional)	
1 teaspoon granulated garlic powder, or 5 cloves fresh garlic, minced or pressed	
2 tablespoons red wine vinegar or freshly squeezed lemon juice, or a combination	
1 teaspoon salt, to taste	

In a bowl, stir together all the ingredients, starting with 1/2 teaspoon salt and adding more to taste. Store in a tightly covered container in the refrigerator for up to 1 week.

Add the flour, salt, yeast, sugar, and olive oil. If using a mixer, use the paddle attachment and mix on the lowest speed for about 1 minute. If mixing by hand, use a large spoon and stir for about 1 minute, until well blended. The dough should be soft, coarse, and very tacky. Let the dough rest for 5 minutes to fully hydrate the flour.

Switch to the dough hook and mix on medium-low speed, or continue mixing by hand, for 3 minutes, until the dough is smoother, soft, supple, and very tacky or slightly sticky.

Follow the instructions on page 68 for shaping, topping, and baking.

HERB OIL	MAKES ABOUT 2 CUPS
2 cups olive oil	2 tablespoons granulated garlic powder, or 10 cloves fresh garlic, pressed and lightly sautéed in $1/2$ cup of the olive oil
2 tablespoons dried basil	
2 tablespoons dried parsley	1 tablespoon kosher salt or coarse sea salt
1 tablespoon dried oregano	$1/4$ teaspoon freshly ground black pepper
1 tablespoon fresh rosemary leaves	1 teaspoon chile flakes (optional)
1 teaspoon dried thyme	1 teaspoon sweet or hot paprika (optional)

In a bowl, whisk together all the ingredients. Let sit at room temperature for 2 hours before using.

SPICY OIL	MAKES 1 CUP
1 cup olive oil	
4 teaspoons sweet or hot paprika	
4 teaspoons chile flakes	
1 large clove garlic, peeled	
$1/4$ teaspoon salt (optional)	

In a saucepan, combine the olive oil, paprika, chile flakes, and garlic and bring to a boil over medium heat. Reduce the heat to low and simmer gently for 10 minutes. Remove from the heat and let cool for 30 minutes. Strain the oil into a jar, add the salt, and let cool completely. Cover and store in the refrigerator for up to 2 weeks.

50% Whole Grain Rustic Bread and Pizza Dough

MAKES 2 TO 3 RUSTIC LOAVES OR 5 PIZZAS

The main difference between the bread and pizza dough is the amount of hydration and the amount of yeast; pizza dough has less water and less yeast than the bread. This formula offers both options, with the amounts of water and yeast for pizza dough appearing after the amounts for bread dough. The sugar and oil are optional, but highly recommended to counteract the bitter tones of the whole wheat flour and to soften the bran.

2$^1/_4$ cups (10 oz / 283 g) whole wheat flour

2$^1/_4$ cups (10 oz / 283 g) unbleached bread flour

1$^3/_4$ teaspoons (0.4 oz / 11 g) salt, or 2$^1/_2$ teaspoons coarse kosher salt

1$^1/_4$ teaspoons (0.14 oz / 4 g) instant yeast; for pizza, use 1 teaspoon (0.11 oz / 3 g)

2 tablespoons (1 oz / 28.5 g) sugar, or 1$^1/_2$ tablespoons honey or agave nectar (optional)

2 cups (16 oz / 454 g) water; for pizza, use 1$^3/_4$ cups plus 1 tablespoon (14.5 oz / 411 g)

2 tablespoons (1 oz / 28.5 g) olive oil (optional)

To make bread using this recipe, follow the instructions for *pain à l'ancienne* (page 52), adding the sugar at the beginning of the process. To make pizza dough, follow the instructions for neo-Neopolitan pizza dough (page 67), again adding the sugar at the beginning.

VARIATIONS

Any whole wheat dough can be turned into a multigrain dough by substituting any combination of flour or meal from other grains for up to 20 percent of the whole wheat flour (by weight). Also, reduce the water by 1 ounce (28.5 g). For instance, you could add a multigrain cereal blend to replace an equal amount of whole wheat flour. If you use more than 20 percent alternate grains, there may not be enough gluten to achieve the necessary structural strength. That said, some people do enjoy experimenting with larger amounts. One solution is to add vital wheat gluten to provide the extra structure. If you do this, don't use more than 2 percent (again, by weight) of the total amount of flour, as it can have a negative impact on both flavor and texture.

100% Whole Grain Rustic Bread and Pizza Dough

In this formula, the amounts of water and yeast for pizza dough appear after the amounts for bread dough. Note that unlike in the 50% whole grain version opposite, the sugar and oil aren't optional; they're definitely needed to counteract the bitter tones of the whole wheat flour and to soften the bran. If you'd like to make a multigrain version, see the variation below.

$5^1/_3$ cups (24 oz / 680 g) whole wheat flour

2 teaspoons (0.5 oz / 14 g) salt, or 1 tablespoon coarse kosher salt

$1^1/_4$ teaspoons (0.14 oz / 4 g) instant yeast; for pizza use
1 teaspoon (0.11 oz / 3 g)

3 tablespoons (1.5 oz / 43 g) sugar, or 2 tablespoons honey
or agave nectar

$2^1/_3$ cups (19 oz / 539 g) water; for pizza, use $2^1/_4$ cups (18 oz / 510 g)

3 tablespoons (1.5 oz / 43 g) olive oil

To make bread using this recipe, follow the instructions for *pain à l'ancienne* (page 52), adding the sugar at the beginning of the process. To make pizza dough, follow the instructions for neo-Neopolitan pizza dough (page 67), again adding the sugar at the beginning of the process.

VARIATIONS

You can make a multigrain variation using 80 percent whole wheat flour and 20 percent (by weight) other whole grain flours in any combination. Just be sure the total weight still adds up to 24 ounces (680 g). Also, reduce the water by 1 ounce (28.5 g).

Bagels

Let's clear something up right away: New York City isn't the only place in the world to get decent, authentic bagels. The truth is, you can make bagels that are just as good at home, no matter where you live. They're one of the simplest breads to make, requiring only flour, water, salt, yeast, and malt—and one secret ingredient: time (in the form of long, slow, cold fermentation). Any decent bagel shop knows this and uses an overnight method to stretch out the fermentation process, releasing all sorts of subtle flavors trapped in the flour. While bagel shops often use a type of high-protein flour not available to home cooks to achieve that distinctively chewy texture, regular, unbleached bread flour can also do the trick. The real key is to use a much lower percentage of water than is used for baguettes and other European hearth breads, producing a stiff dough that can stand up to a dunking in boiling water before going into the oven. More than any ingredient or other aspect of the method, this boiling step is what defines the uniqueness of the bagel.

That said, bagels do usually feature one other distinctive ingredient: barley malt. While this may seem like an exotic, hard-to-find product, it's actually commonly available at most supermarkets, usually labeled "barley malt syrup." If you can't find it, simply substitute an equal amount of honey. Your bagels might not have that malty flavor, but they'll still be better than almost any bagel you can buy.

One final note: If you like bagels but don't want to set up the boiling operation for just six of them, feel free to double the size of the batch and bake enough to freeze for future use.

DOUGH

1 tablespoon (0.75 oz / 21 g) barley malt syrup, honey, or rice syrup, or 1 teaspoon (0.25 oz / 7 g) diastatic malt powder

1 teaspoon (0.11 oz / 3 g) instant yeast

1^1/$_2$ teaspoons (0.37 oz / 10.5 g) salt, or 2^1/$_2$ teaspoons coarse kosher salt

1 cup plus 2 tablespoons (9 oz / 255 g) lukewarm water (about 95°F or 35°C)

3^1/$_2$ cups (16 oz / 454 g) unbleached bread flour

2 to 3 quarts (64 to 96 oz / 181 to 272 g) water

1$\frac{1}{2}$ tablespoons (1 oz / 28.5 g) barley malt syrup or honey (optional)

1 tablespoon (0.5 oz / 14 g) baking soda

1 teaspoon (0.25 oz / 7 g) salt, or 1$\frac{1}{2}$ teaspoons coarse kosher salt

DO AHEAD

To make the dough, stir the malt syrup, yeast, and salt into the lukewarm water. Place the flour into a mixing bowl and pour in the malt syrup mixture. If using a mixer, use the dough hook and mix on the lowest speed for 3 minutes. If mixing by hand, use a large, sturdy spoon and stir for about 3 minutes, until well blended. The dough should form a stiff, coarse ball, and the flour should be fully hydrated; if it isn't, stir in a little more water. Let the dough rest for 5 minutes.

Resume mixing with the dough hook on the lowest speed for another 3 minutes or transfer to a very lightly floured work surface and knead by hand for about 3 minutes to smooth out the dough and develop the gluten. The dough should be stiff yet supple, with a satiny, barely tacky feel. If the dough seems too soft or overly tacky, mix or knead in a little more flour.

Place the dough in a clean, lightly oiled bowl, cover the bowl tightly with plastic wrap, and let the dough rise at room temperature for 1 hour.

When you're ready to shape the bagels, prepare a sheet pan by lining it with parchment paper or a silicone mat, then misting it with spray oil or lightly coating it with oil. Divide the dough into 6 to 8 equal pieces. (A typical bagel is about 4 ounces or 113 grams before baking, but you can make them smaller. If you make more than 6 bagels, you may need to prepare 2 sheet pans.) Form each piece into a loose ball by rolling it on a clean, dry work surface with a cupped hand. (Don't use any flour on the work surface. If the dough slides around and won't ball up, wipe the surface with a damp paper towel and try again; the slight bit of moisture will provide enough traction for the dough to form into a ball.) There are two methods to shape the balls into bagels.

The first method is to poke a hole through the center of the ball to create a donut shape. Holding the dough with both thumbs in the hole, rotate the dough with your hands, gradually stretching it to create a hole about 2 inches in diameter.

The second method, preferred by professional bagel makers, is to use both hands (and a fair amount of pressure) to roll the ball into a rope about 8 inches long on a clean, dry work

surface. (Again, wipe the surface with a damp towel, if necessary, to create sufficient friction on the work surface.) Taper the rope slightly at each end and moisten the last inch or so of the ends. Place one end of the dough in the palm of your hand and wrap the rope around your hand to complete the circle, going between your thumb and forefinger and then all the way around. The ends should overlap by about 2 inches. Squeeze the overlapping ends together by closing your hand, then press the seam into the work surface, rolling it back and forth a few times to seal. Remove the dough from your hand, squeezing it to even out the thickness if need be and creating a hole of about 2 inches in diameter.

Place each shaped bagel on the prepared sheet pan, then mist with spray oil or brush with a light coating of oil. Cover the entire pan with plastic wrap and refrigerate overnight or for up to 2 days. (You can also proof the full piece of dough in the oiled bowl overnight and then shape the bagels on baking day, 60 to 90 minutes before boiling and baking them, or as soon as they pass the float test.)

ON BAKING DAY

Remove the bagels from the refrigerator 60 to 90 minutes before you plan to bake them, and if you plan to top them with dried onion or garlic, rehydrate those ingredients (see the variations on page 78). Immediately check whether the bagels are ready for baking using the "float test": Place one of the bagels in a small bowl of cold water. If it sinks and doesn't float back to the surface, shake it off, return it to the pan, and wait for another 15 to 20 minutes, then test it again. When one bagel passes the float test, they're all ready to be boiled. If they pass the float test before you are ready to boil and bake them, return them to the refrigerator so they don't overproof. About 30 minutes before baking, preheat the oven to 500°F (260°C) and gather and prepare your garnishes (seeds, onions, garlic, and so on).

To make the poaching liquid, fill a pot with 2 to 3 quarts (64 to 96 oz / 181 to 272 g) of water, making sure the water is at least 4 inches deep. Cover, bring to a boil, then lower the heat to maintain at a simmer. Stir in the malt syrup, baking soda, and salt.

Gently lower each bagel into the simmering poaching liquid, adding as many as will comfortably fit in the pot. They should all float to the surface within 15 seconds. After 1 minute, use a slotted spoon to turn each bagel over. Poach for another 30 to 60 seconds, then use the slotted spoon to transfer it back to the pan, domed side up. (It's important that the parchment paper be lightly oiled, or the paper will glue itself to the dough as the bagels bake.) Sprinkle on a generous amount of whatever toppings you like as soon as the bagels come out of the water (except cinnamon sugar; see the variation on page 78 for details).

Transfer the pan of bagels to the oven, then lower the oven heat to 450°F (232°C).

Bake for 8 minutes, then rotate the pan and check the underside of the bagels. If they're getting too dark, place another pan under the baking sheet. (Doubling the pan will insulate the first baking sheet.) Bake for another 8 to 12 minutes, until the bagels are a golden brown.

Cool on a wire rack for at least 30 minutes before slicing or serving.

VARIATIONS

You can replace any amount of the bread flour with an equal amount of whole grain flour (by weight), such as wheat or rye. If you do so, increase the water in the dough by 1 tablespoon (0.5 oz / 14 g) for every 2 ounces (56.5 g) of whole grain flour you substitute.

Top your bagels with any combination of the following garnishes: poppy seeds, sesame seeds, coarse salt, or rehydrated dried onions or garlic. (Soak dried onions or garlic in water to cover for at least 1 hour before applying.) The toppings will stick even better if you first brush the top of each bagel with an egg white wash made by whisking 1 egg white with 1 tablespoon (0.5 oz / 14 g) of water. If using coarse salt as a garnish, remember that a little goes a long way.

For raisin bagels, mix in $1^1/3$ cups (8 oz / 227 g) of raisins during the final 2 minutes of mixing and, if you like cinnamon, stir $^1/_2$ teaspoon (0.14 oz / 4 g) of ground cinnamon into the flour before you start mixing. When the bagels come out of the oven, brush the tops with melted butter and dip the top into a bed of cinnamon sugar to give it a very tasty cinnamon crust. You can make cinnamon sugar by whisking 2 tablespoons (1.6 oz / 44 g) of ground cinnamon into $^1/_2$ cup (4 oz / 113 g) of granulated sugar.

Clockwise from top: wild rice and onion bread (page 113); soft rye sandwich bread (page 109), shown marbled; many-seed bread (page 102); struan (page 91)

CHAPTER 4

Enriched Breads

Enriched breads are those made with moderate amounts of fat, sugar, eggs, and dairy products. (In chapter 5, Rich Breads, the formulas contain much higher amounts of these enrichments.) These breads are soft and slightly sweet and tend to be used for sandwich loaves and soft rolls. Crackers and pretzels often fall into this category, as well, so you'll find recipes for them in this chapter, too.

You may wonder what these enrichments do to bread. Fats tenderize the final product and lock in moisture, which softens bread and extends its shelf life. Fat also enhances flavor even when it has little or no flavor of its own. Butter and olive oil, which do have delightful flavors, provide their own flavors as a bonus. Sugars, including those in liquid form, such as honey and syrups, also enhance softness and aid in moisture retention. However, their sweetness is probably their most important quality in bread—not just for flavor, but also for color. Caramelized sugar plays an important role in the browning of crust. Eggs and dairy products provide flavor, natural sugars, nutritional value in the form of protein and minerals, and sometimes fat. So to a certain extent, eggs and dairy products have functions similar to fat and sugar. Egg yolks are high in lecithin, which functions as an emulsifier, and are thus very useful in creaming ingredients together when making quick breads and cakes. By binding fats and liquid together, lecithin helps trap air to make lighter breads.

Armed with this background (knowledge of the functionality of ingredients is an important tool for bakers), the following pages offer a few of my favorite enriched bread products. Enjoy!

THREE 100% WHOLE GRAIN BREADS

One of the most encouraging recent dietary trends is a return to eating more whole grain bread, and more whole grain products in general—and for good reason. Whole grain breads are by far the most nutritious, not only because of the fiber and nutrients provided by the bran and germ, but also because they're digested more slowly, providing more stable energy instead of a spike followed by a crash. White flour, on the other hand, is absorbed by the body much more rapidly.

In my previous book, *Peter Reinhart's Whole Grain Breads*, I introduced a method of mixing and fermenting dough that brought two artisan techniques together in a new way. I called it the epoxy method because every recipe uses two pre-doughs: one pre-femented, such as a sourdough starter, and the other not fermented, such as a soaker or a mash. The purpose of this method was to evoke the full potential of flavor trapped in the grain by using enzymes and fermentation to develop the flavor, then bringing the pieces together on the second day in a final mix. The goal was to create extremely healthful breads that also tasted great.

For this book, I've modified the epoxy method to simplify it and use the same overnight method employed in most of the recipes in this book. After all, holding the dough overnight uses both parts of the epoxy method: the pre-ferment and the soaker. However, in order to retain enough leavening power in the yeast without adding a second mix on the second day, as in the epoxy method, the dough must be fairly wet and contain a higher percentage of yeast. The following three formulas—one for enriched, soft sandwich-style bread and the other two for lean, slightly enriched hearth bread—can be modified into many variations by adding other grains, as detailed in the sidebar.

Everyday 100% Whole Wheat Sandwich Bread

This bread can be used for anything that you'd make with white bread, including buns, rolls, and toast. You can use either traditional "red" whole wheat flour or the new "white" whole wheat that is lighter in color and slightly less bitter. If you choose the honey or agave nectar option in this recipe, you'll need more flour than if you use sugar, probably an extra $3^1/_2$ to 7 tablespoons (1 to 2 oz). Assess the texture as you mix and adjust accordingly.

$6^1/_4$ cups (28 oz / 794 g) whole wheat flour

2 teaspoons (0.5 oz / 14 g) salt, or 1 tablespoon coarse kosher salt

5 tablespoons (2.5 oz / 71 g) granulated or brown sugar, or
$3^1/_2$ tablespoons honey or agave nectar

1 egg (1.75 oz / 50 g)

$^1/_4$ cup (2 oz / 56.5 g) vegetable oil

$1^1/_4$ cups (10 oz / 283 g) lukewarm water (about 95°F or 35°C)

$1^1/_4$ cups (10 oz / 283 g) lukewarm milk (any kind; at about 95°F or 35°C)

$1^1/_2$ tablespoons (0.5 oz / 14 g) instant yeast

Multigrain Variations

Replace up to 5.5 ounces (156 g) of the whole wheat flour with the same weight of any of the following ingredients, in any combination:

* Whole rye flour, rye meal, rye flakes (whole or ground)

* Uncooked cornmeal or cooked grits or polenta

* Oatmeal flakes, whole or ground

* Amaranth

* Uncooked ground quinoa or cooked whole quinoa

* Whole or ground flaxseeds (no more than 1 ounce or 28.5 g)

* Cooked brown rice, bulgur, barley

In a mixing bowl, whisk the flour, salt, and sugar together (if using honey or agave nectar, dissolve it in the lukewarm water instead). In a separate bowl, whisk the egg and oil together. Separately, combine the water and milk, then whisk in the yeast until dissolved.

Add the egg mixture and the water mixture to the dry ingredients. If using a mixer, use the paddle attachment and mix on the lowest speed for 1 minute. If mixing by hand, use a large spoon and stir for 1 about minute. The dough should be wet and coarse. Let the dough rest for 5 minutes to fully hydrate the flour.

Switch to the dough hook and mix on medium-low speed, or continue mixing by hand, for 2 minutes. The dough will firm up slightly and become smoother. If it's still very wet, add more flour; if it's very stiff, add a little more water, 1 tablespoon at a time. The dough should be very supple and slightly sticky. Continue to mix with the dough hook on medium-low speed, or mix by hand for 4 minutes more, increasing the speed to medium-high or stirring more vigorously for the final 20 seconds to develop and organize the gluten. The dough will still be slightly sticky but will also feel stronger and more elastic.

Transfer the dough to a lightly floured work surface with a wet bowl scraper and knead by hand for a final few seconds, working in more flour or water as needed so that the dough is very supple and pliable and slightly sticky; then form the dough into a ball. Do a stretch and fold, either on the work surface or in the bowl, reaching under the front end of the dough, stretching it out, then folding it back onto the top of the dough. Do this from the back end and then from each side, then flip the dough over and tuck it into a ball. Cover the dough and let it rest for 10 minutes. Repeat this entire process two more times, completing all repetitions within 30 minutes.

Place the dough in a clean, lightly oiled bowl large enough to hold the dough when it doubles in size. Cover the bowl tightly with plastic wrap, then immediately refrigerate overnight or for up to 4 days. (If you plan to bake the dough in batches over different days, you can portion the dough and place it into two or more oiled bowls at this stage.)

Remove the dough from the refrigerator about 3 hours before you plan to bake. Transfer the dough to a lightly floured work surface and divide it into two equal pieces for loaves or small pieces for rolls, about 2 ounces each. Shape the dough into sandwich loaves (see page 23), freestanding loaves (see page 20), or rolls (see page 25). For sandwich loaves, place the dough in greased 4¹/₂ by 8¹/₂-inch loaf pans. For freestanding loaves or rolls, line a sheet pan with parchment paper or a silicone mat and proof the dough on the pan. Mist the dough with spray oil and cover loosely with plastic wrap, then let the dough rise at room temperature for 2 to 3 hours, until increased to about $1^1/_2$ times its original size. In loaf pans, the dough should dome about 1 inch above the rim.

About 15 minutes before baking, preheat the oven to 350°F (177°C). If making rolls, brush the dough with egg wash (see page 135) prior to baking. (This isn't necessary for loaves.)

Bake loaves for 20 minutes, then rotate; rotate rolls after 10 minutes. The total baking time is 40 to 55 minutes for loaves, and only about 20 minutes for rolls. The bread is done when the top and sides are a deep, rich brown; the loaf sounds hollow when thumped on the bottom; and the internal temperature is above 185°F (85°C) in the center.

Remove from the pans and cool for at least 20 minutes for rolls and at least 1 hour for loaves before slicing or serving.

VARIATIONS

For a stronger, more elastic dough, add 2 tablespoons (0.5 oz / 14 g) of vital wheat gluten (sometimes called pure wheat gluten). This will create a lighter loaf with larger air pockets. Increase the water by $^1/_4$ cup (2 oz / 56.5 g).

You can also omit the milk and replace it with more water, but milk makes the bread a little more tender and golden. Another option is to substitute soy milk or rice milk.

You can easily make a multigrain version of this bread. As long as you use whole wheat flour for at least 80 percent of the total flour, there will be enough gluten to support the loaf. This means you can replace up to 20 percent of the whole wheat flour with an equal amount of other grains (by weight), in a variety of forms, including rye flour, multigrain cereal blends, cornmeal, and flaked or rolled grains like oats or triticale flakes. (If using flakes, you can use them in flaked form or grind them into flour in a seed grinder or blender.) You can also use small-seeded "grains" like amaranth, chia seeds, millet, and quinoa. Amaranth and chia are about the only grains that can go into a loaf whole, without being rolled or ground into flakes, meal, or flour. Slightly larger grains, like millet, quinoa, and corn grits, can also be left whole if you like the crunch they provide. If you want to use larger grains like rice, rye, barley, or wheat in their whole form, thoroughly cook them first, as they won't hydrate in the dough and could crack a tooth.

To win someone over from white bread to 100 percent whole grain bread, it may help to have a transitional version that bridges the gap. You can replace some of the whole wheat flour in this recipe with an equal amount of unbleached bread flour (by weight) to make a lighter loaf. Reduce the amount of water by about $^1/_2$ tablespoon (0.25 oz or 6 g) for every 1 ounce (28.5 g) of bread flour you use.

100% Whole Wheat Hearth Bread

MAKES 2 LOAVES

No bread is as good for us as one made completely from whole grains. The challenge with 100 percent whole grain breads, though, is achieving an open crumb and airy texture. The bran fiber in the whole grain flour, while extremely beneficial in our diet, acts like little razors in the dough, cutting the thin gluten strands. This makes it difficult for the loaf to rise as high as white flour loaves. The antidote is to use a higher percentage of hydration, which counteracts some of the stiffness caused by the bran, softening the fiber and promoting additional oven spring. The dough will seem very soft when it is first mixed but will gradually firm up as it ferments, as the fiber slowly swells as it absorbs the water. As more and more of us make the switch to whole grains, this bread will become a valuable addition to your repertoire. For a variety of options in making this bread, see page 83, where you'll find multigrain suggestions, guidelines for making transitional breads with less than 100 percent whole grains, and more.

6$^1/_4$ cups (28 oz / 794 g) whole wheat flour

2 teaspoons (0.5 oz / 14 g) salt, or 1 tablespoon coarse kosher salt

2 tablespoons (1 oz / 28.5 g) granulated sugar or brown sugar, or 1$^1/_2$ tablespoons honey or agave nectar

1 tablespoon (0.33 oz / 9 g) instant yeast

2$^3/_4$ cups (22 oz / 624 g) lukewarm water (about 95°F or 35°C)

2 tablespoons (1 oz / 28.5 g) vegetable oil

DO AHEAD

In a mixing bowl, whisk the flour, salt, and sugar together (if using honey or agave nectar, dissolve it in the lukewarm water instead). Stir the yeast into the lukewarm water, whisk to dissolve the yeast, then stir in the oil.

Add the water mixture to the flour mixture. If using a mixer, use the paddle attachment and mix on the lowest speed for 1 minute. If mixing by hand, use a large spoon and stir for about 1 minute. The dough should be wet and coarse. Let the dough sit for 5 minutes to fully hydrate the flour.

Switch to the dough hook and mix on medium-low speed, or continue mixing by hand, for 2 minutes. The dough will firm up slightly and become smoother. If it's very stiff, add a little more water, 1 teaspoon at a time. The dough should be very supple and slightly sticky. Continue to mix with the dough hook on medium-low speed, or to mix by hand, for 4 minutes more, increasing the speed to medium-high or stirring more vigorously for the final 20 seconds to develop and organize the gluten. The dough will still be slightly sticky but will also feel stronger and more elastic.

Transfer the dough to a lightly floured work surface with a wet bowl scraper. With wet or oiled hands, reach under one end of the dough, stretch it out, then fold it back onto the top of the dough. Do this from the back end and then from each side, then flip the dough over and tuck it into a ball. The dough should be slightly firmer, though still very soft and fragile. Place the dough in a clean, lightly oiled bowl, cover, and let sit at room temperature for 10 minutes. Repeat this entire process three more times, completing all repetitions within 40 minutes.

After the final stretch and fold, immediately cover the bowl tightly and refrigerate the dough overnight or for up to 4 days. The dough will rise to about double, and possibly triple, its original size within 8 to 12 hours in the refrigerator. (If you plan to bake the dough in batches over different days, you can portion the dough and place it into two or more oiled bowls at this stage.)

ON BAKING DAY

Remove the dough from the refrigerator about 3 hours before you plan to bake. Transfer the dough to a lightly floured work surface and divide it into two equal pieces for loaves or small pieces for rolls. Shape the cold dough into freestanding loaves (see page 20) or rolls (see page 25). You can use *bannetons*, *couches*, or the back of a sheet pan lined with parchment paper to proof the bread. Mist the dough with spray oil and cover loosely with plastic wrap, then let the dough rise at room temperature for 2 to 3 hours, until increased to $1^{1}/_{2}$ times its original size.

Preheat the oven to 500°F (260°C) and prepare it for hearth baking (see page 30). Uncover the dough 15 minutes before baking and score it with a sharp serrated knife or razor blade (scoring rolls is optional).

Transfer the dough to the oven, pour 1 cup of hot water into the steam pan, and lower the oven temperature to 425°F (218°C).

Bake loaves for 15 minutes, then rotate the pan; rotate rolls after 10 minutes. The total baking time is 35 to 45 minutes for loaves, and only 20 to 22 minutes for rolls. The bread is done when the top and sides are a deep, rich brown; the loaf sounds hollow when thumped on the bottom; and the internal temperature is above 195°F (91°C) in the center. For a crisper crust, leave the bread in the oven for 5 to 10 minutes after you turn off the oven.

Cool on a wire rack for at least 20 minutes for rolls and 45 minutes for loaves before slicing or serving.

100% Whole Wheat Sourdough Hearth Bread

MAKES 2 LOAVES

As with other sourdough recipes in this book, you have two options with this recipe. For a "purist" version, omit the instant yeast from the final dough. For a mixed method, which will rise more quickly but lack some of the sour flavor, include the instant yeast. The optional oil helps lubricate and soften the bran fiber in whole grain bread. For a variety of other options in making this bread, see page 83, where you'll find multigrain suggestions, guidelines for making transitional breads with less than 100 percent whole grains, and more.

WHOLE WHEAT SOURDOUGH STARTER

$^1/_4$ cup (2 oz / 56.5 g) mother starter (page 42), cold or at room temperature

$1^1/_3$ cups (6 oz / 170 g) whole wheat flour

$^1/_2$ cup plus 1 tablespoon (4.5 oz / 128 g) lukewarm water (about 95°F or 35°C)

DOUGH

All of the whole wheat sourdough starter (12.5 oz / 354 g)

$1^1/_2$ tablespoons (1 oz / 28.5 g) honey or agave nectar, or 2 tablespoons sugar

$1^1/_2$ cups (12 oz / 340 g) lukewarm water (about 95°F or 35°C)

2 tablespoons (1 oz / 28.5 g) vegetable oil (optional)

$3^1/_2$ cups (16 oz / 454 g) whole wheat flour

2 teaspoons (0.5 oz / 14 g) salt, or 1 tablespoon coarse kosher salt

$1^1/_2$ teaspoons (0.17 oz / 5 g) instant yeast (optional)

DO AHEAD

To make the starter, combine all of the ingredients in a mixing bowl. If using a mixer, use the paddle attachment and mix on the lowest speed for 1 minute, then increase to medium speed for about 30 seconds. If mixing by hand, stir for about 2 minutes, until well blended. The starter should feel doughlike and tacky or slightly sticky; if not, stir in additional flour or water as needed.

Transfer the starter to a lightly floured work surface and knead for about 30 seconds. Place it in a clean, lightly oiled bowl, cover the bowl loosely, and leave at room temperature for 6 to 8 hours, until the starter increases to about $1^1/_2$ times its original size. Use the starter immediately to make the final dough, or refrigerate overnight or for up to 4 days.

To make the dough, cut the starter into 10 or 12 pieces and put them in a mixing bowl. Dissolve the honey in the warm water (if using sugar rather than honey, mix it in with the flour and salt), then stir in the oil and pour the mixture into the mixing bowl. Stir to soften the starter, then add the flour and salt, along with the instant yeast (unless making the "purist" version). If using a mixer, use the paddle attachment and mix on the lowest speed for 1 minute, or stir with a large spoon for about 1 minute, to evenly distribute the ingredients and create a wet, coarse dough. Let the dough sit for 5 minutes to fully hydrate the flour.

Switch to the dough hook and mix on medium-low speed, or continue mixing by hand, for 2 minutes. The dough will firm up slightly and become smoother. If it's very stiff, add a

little more water, 1 teaspoon at a time. The dough should be very supple and slightly sticky. Continue to mix with the dough hook on medium-low speed, or mix by hand, for 4 minutes more, increasing the speed to medium-high or kneading more vigorously for the final 20 seconds to develop and organize the gluten. The dough will still be slightly sticky but will also feel stronger and more elastic.

Transfer the dough to a lightly floured work surface with a wet bowl scraper. With wet or oiled hands, reach under one end of the dough, stretch it out, then fold it back onto the top of the dough. Do this from the back end and then from each side, then flip the dough over and tuck it into a ball. The dough should be slightly firmer, though still very soft and fragile. Place the dough in a clean, lightly oiled bowl, cover, and let sit at room temperature for 10 minutes. Repeat this entire process three more times, completing all repetitions within 40 minutes.

After the final stretch and fold, immediately cover the bowl tightly and refrigerate the dough overnight or for up to 4 days (for the "purist" version, leave the dough out for 2 to 3 hours before refrigerating). The dough will rise to about double, and possibly triple, its original size within 8 to 12 hours in the refrigerator. (If you plan to bake the dough in batches over different days, you can portion the dough and place it into two or more oiled bowls at this stage.)

ON BAKING DAY

Remove the dough from the refrigerator about 3 hours before you plan to bake (or 4 hours before for the "purist" version). Transfer the dough to a lightly floured work surface and divide it into two equal pieces for loaves or small pieces for rolls. Shape the dough as freestanding loaves (see page 20) or rolls (see page 25). You can use *bannetons*, *couches*, or the back of a sheet pan lined with parchment paper to proof the bread. Mist the dough with spray oil and cover loosely with plastic wrap, then let the dough rise at room temperature for 2 to 3 hours (up to 4 hours for the "purist" version), until increased to 1$^{1}/_{2}$ times its original size.

Preheat the oven to 500°F (260°C) and prepare it for hearth baking (see page 30). Uncover the dough 15 minutes before baking and score it with a sharp serrated knife or razor blade (scoring rolls is optional).

Transfer the dough to the oven, pour 1 cup of hot water into the steam pan, and lower the temperature to 425°F (218°C).

Bake the loaves for 15 minutes, then rotate the pan; rotate rolls after 10 minutes. The total baking time is 35 to 45 minutes for loaves, and only 20 to 22 minutes for rolls. The bread is done when the top and sides are a deep, rich brown; the loaf sounds hollow when thumped on the bottom; and the internal temperature is above 195°F (91°C) in the center. For a crisper crust, leave the bread in the oven for 5 to 10 minutes after you turn the off oven.

Cool on a wire rack for at least 20 minutes for rolls and 45 minutes for loaves before slicing or serving.

Struan

MAKES 2 LOAVES OR MANY ROLLS

Every book I write has yet another variation of this soft, enriched multigrain loaf, my all-time favorite bread. The name comes from western Scotland, probably the town called Struanmoor, on the Isle of Skye, and also from a Gaelic clan name that means "a convergence of streams." It was originally conceived of as a once-a-year harvest bread, incorporating whatever grains and seeds were available from the previous day's harvest. Because the notion of a harvest bread offers a great deal of formula flexibility, I'm always looking for ways to push the *struan* envelope in search of better or easier versions.

This recipe is very similar to the version I originally made at my bakery, Brother Juniper's, and it was by far the most popular bread we made. This time around, I've taken advantage of the overnight, cold fermentation method to come up with a recipe that's more flexible, particularly in regard to time options. This is the ultimate toasting bread. There's something about the combination of ingredients that creates the perfect balance of flavor and texture when toasted and spread with butter, jam, or both. It also works beautifully as a sandwich bread with fillings like tuna salad, chicken salad, or egg salad. You can reduce the amount of sugar or honey if you prefer, but I like the sweetness of this bread and think the combination of brown sugar and honey enhances the toasting qualities. Still, sweetness is a very personal matter, so follow your heart and your palate.

5 cups (22.5 oz / 638 g) unbleached bread flour

$1/4$ cup (1.5 oz / 42.5 g) coarse cornmeal (polenta grind)

$1/4$ cup (1 oz / 28.5 g) rolled oats

3 tablespoons (0.75 oz / 21 g) wheat bran or oat bran

$1/2$ cup (2 oz / 56.5 g) cooked brown rice

$1/4$ cup (2 oz / 56.5 g) brown sugar

$2^{1}/2$ teaspoons (0.66 oz / 19 g) salt, or $3^{1}/2$ teaspoons coarse kosher salt

2 tablespoons (0.66 oz / 19 g) instant yeast

$1^{1}/2$ tablespoons (1 oz / 28.5 g) honey or agave nectar

$1^{1}/2$ cups (12 oz / 340 g) lukewarm water (about 95°F or 35°C)

$1/2$ cup (4 oz / 113 g) lukewarm buttermilk, yogurt, or any other milk (about 95°F or 35°C)

Poppy seeds or sesame seeds, for garnish (optional)

Combine the flour, cornmeal, oats, bran, rice, sugar, salt, yeast, honey, water, and milk in a mixing bowl. If using a mixer, use the paddle attachment and mix on the lowest speed for 2 minutes. If mixing by hand, use a large spoon and stir for about 2 minutes. The dough will be sticky, coarse, and shaggy. Let the dough rest for 5 minutes to fully hydrate the flour.

Once again, mix on the slowest speed with the paddle attachment, or by hand using a large spoon, for 2 minutes more to further develop the dough. Add flour as needed to keep the dough together, but it should still be soft and very tacky or slightly sticky. (In the unlikely event that the dough is too stiff, work in a little more water.)

Use a bowl scraper to transfer the dough to a lightly floured work surface, then dust the top of the dough with flour. Lightly knead the dough for 2 to 3 minutes, adding more flour as needed to prevent sticking. The dough will still be soft and sticky but should hold together to form a soft, supple ball. With wet or oiled hands, reach under one end of the dough, stretch it out, then fold it back onto the top of the dough. Do this from the back end and then from each side, then flip the dough over and tuck it into a ball. The dough should be slightly firmer, though still very soft and fragile. Place the dough in a clean, lightly oiled bowl, cover, and let sit at room temperature for 10 minutes. Repeat this entire process three more times, completing all repetitions within 40 minutes.

After the final stretch and fold, place the dough in a clean, lightly oiled bowl, cover the bowl tightly with plastic wrap, and refrigerate overnight or for up to 5 days. (If you plan to bake the dough in batches over different days, you can portion the dough and place it into two or more oiled bowls at this stage.)

Remove the dough from the refrigerator about 2 hours before you plan to bake. Shape the cold dough into one or more sandwich loaves (see page 23), using 28 ounces (794 g) of dough for 4 1/2 by 8-inch loaf pans and 36 ounces (1.02 kg) of dough for 5 by 9-inch pans; into freestanding loaves of any size, which you can shape as *bâtards* (see page 21), baguettes (see page 22), or *boules* (see page 20); or into rolls (see page 25), using about 2 ounces (56.5 g) of dough per roll. When shaping, use only as much flour on the work surface as necessary to keep the dough from sticking. For sandwich loaves, proof the dough in greased loaf pans. For freestanding loaves and rolls, line a sheet pan with parchment paper or a silicone mat and proof the dough on the pan.

Brush the top of the dough with water and sprinkle with poppy (or sesame) seeds, then mist with spray oil and cover loosely with plastic wrap. Let the dough rise at room temperature for $1^1/_2$ to 2 hours, until increased to about $1^1/_2$ times its original size. In loaf pans, the dough should dome at least 1 inch above the rim.

About 15 minutes before baking, preheat the oven to 350°F (177°C), 300°F (149°C) for a convection oven.

Bake the loaves for 20 minutes, then rotate the pan; rotate rolls after 10 minutes. The total baking time is 45 to 60 minutes for loaves, and only 20 to 25 minutes for rolls. The bread is done when it has a rich golden color, the loaf sounds hollow when thumped on the bottom, and the internal temperature is above 185°F (85°C) in the center.

Cool for at least 20 minutes for rolls and 1 hour for large loaves before slicing or serving.

VARIATIONS

You can substitute almost any cooked grain, such as bulgur, millet, or quinoa, for the brown rice. Just don't use white rice, as it tends to stand out too much and draw attention to itself, and don't use cooked grain that's more than 5 days old unless it's been kept in the freezer. If you don't want to take the time to cook grains for this recipe, you can make the bread without this ingredient, but don't increase the amount of the uncooked grains to compensate.

In place of the oats, cornmeal, and bran, you can use commercial multigrain blends, such as ten-grain or twelve-grain cereal. Simply replace the 3.25 ounces (92 g) combined weight of those grains with an equal amount of any multigrain blend. Alternatively, you can replace any one of those grains with an equal amount (by weight) of multigrain blend.

If you want to make a sourdough version, add 4 ounces (113 g) of mother starter to the recipe without making any other changes. Don't change the amount of instant yeast; yes, it is a lot of yeast, but it's necessary.

Challah

This dough is distinctive because of its generous use of eggs, which give it a beautiful golden color. This type of dough is most familiar as challah, in a braided form as the table bread for the Jewish Sabbath meal. But enriched egg breads have been made by bakers of many cultures for centuries, and they aren't always braided. If you like the flavor and texture of this bread, feel free to use it to make any number of other baked goods, from dinner rolls to sweet cinnamon buns, and even yeasted coffee cake and sweet or savory swirl breads, like babka or cheese rolls. You can use either an egg white or a whole egg in the egg wash. The whole egg will create a darker crust.

2$^1/_4$ cups (18 oz / 510 g) lukewarm water (about 95°F or 35°C)
1$^1/_2$ tablespoons (0.5 oz / 14 g) instant yeast
8 to 10 egg yolks (6 oz / 170 g), depending on weight
5 tablespoons (2.5 oz / 71 g) vegetable oil
6 tablespoons (3 oz / 85 g) sugar, or 4$^1/_2$ tablespoons honey or agave nectar
1 tablespoon (0.75 oz / 21 g) vanilla extract (optional)
7$^1/_2$ cups (34 oz / 964 g) unbleached bread flour
2$^1/_2$ teaspoons (0.66 oz / 19 g) salt, or 4 teaspoons coarse kosher salt
1 egg white or whole egg, for egg wash
2 tablespoons water, for egg wash
2 tablespoons poppy seeds, sesame seeds, or a combination, for garnish (optional)

DO AHEAD

Combine the water and yeast in a mixing bowl and stir with a whisk to dissolve. Add the egg yolks, oil, sugar, and vanilla and whisk lightly to break up the egg yolks, then add the flour and salt. If using a mixer, use the paddle attachment and mix on the lowest speed for 2 minutes. If mixing by hand, use a large spoon and stir for about 2 minutes. The dough should be coarse and shaggy. Let the dough rest for 5 minutes.

Switch to the dough hook and mix on medium-low speed, or continue to mix by hand using a large, wet spoon, for 4 minutes.

Use a bowl scraper to transfer the dough to a lightly floured work surface, then dust the top of the dough with flour. Lightly knead for 1 to 2 minutes, adding more flour as needed to prevent sticking. The dough should be soft, supple, and tacky but not sticky. Form the dough into a ball, place it in a clean, lightly oiled bowl, and cover the bowl with plastic wrap. Immediately refrigerate the dough overnight or for up to 4 days. It will double in size as it cools. (If you plan to bake the dough in batches over different days, you can portion the dough and place it into two or more oiled bowls at this stage.)

ON BAKING DAY

Remove the dough from the refrigerator about 2 hours and 10 minutes before you plan to bake. Transfer it to a lightly floured work surface and cut it into the desired number of pieces to make strands for braiding, making sure all of the pieces are the same weight. Flatten each piece with your hand, then roll the pieces into a cigar or torpedo shape. After doing this with each piece, return to the first one and roll it out into a rope 10 to 14 inches long. (The bigger the piece of dough, the longer the rope.) Make sure each rope is the same length. See opposite for braiding instructions. Once the loaves are braided, transfer them to a sheet pan lined with parchment paper or a silicone mat.

Make an egg wash by combining the egg white (or a whole egg) and the 2 tablespoons of water and whisking briskly until thoroughly combined. Brush the entire visible surface of the loaves with the egg wash, then refrigerate any remaining egg wash and let the loaves rise, uncovered, at room temperature for about 1 hour; they won't rise very much during this time. Brush with the egg wash again, then sprinkle on the optional seeds. A combination of poppy and sesame looks very impressive. Let the loaves rise at room temperature for about 1 hour, or until increased to about $1^1/_2$ times their original size.

About 15 minutes before baking, preheat the oven to 350°F (177°C), or 300°F (149°C) for a convection oven.

Bake for about 20 minutes, then rotate the pan and bake for another 15 to 30 minutes, until the loaves sound hollow when thumped on the bottom and the internal temperature is about 190°F (88°C) in the center. If you used a whole egg in the egg wash, the crust will get darker than with an egg white wash; don't be fooled into thinking the bread is done until it passes the thump and temperature test. The crust of the loaf will seem hard when it first comes out of the oven, but it will soften as it cools.

Cool on a wire rack for at least 45 minutes before slicing or serving.

If you want to use whole eggs instead of yolks in the dough, reduce the water by 2 tablespoons (1 oz / 28.5 g) per egg. The yolks are the key to the attractive color and also make a major contribution to the soft texture because they add fat and lecithin, which tenderize the bread. The whites add protein; while that's a good thing, they also dry out the bread. Also, feel free to add another tablespoon or so of honey or sugar if you prefer a sweeter bread.

Braided Loaves

You can make braided breads with 2, 3, 4, 5, or 6 strands—or more. The most important principle in braiding loaves is to be sure each strand is the same weight and length. If you don't have a scale, estimate the size as closely as possible. Also keep in mind that the position numbers refer to the actual position of the strands on the counter, starting from your left, rather than to the particular strands; in other words, the number of a given strand changes as it's moved during the braiding process. To form the strands, use the same gentle rocking motion as for shaping baguettes. For all braids, place the prettiest side up when you transfer to the baking sheet, then cover and proof.

To shape a 2-braid loaf, lay 2 strands of equal weight and length on the work surface, perpendicular to one another and crossed in the center. Take both ends of the strand that's underneath and cross them over to the opposite sides. Cross the ends of the other strand in the same way. Continue crossing and alternating until you get to the ends of the strands, then pinch the tips together at each end to seal off the ends. Lay the braid on its side.

To shape a 3-braid loaf, lay 3 equal strands side by side, parallel to one another. Beginning in the middle of the loaf, overlap one of the outside strands over the middle strand, then take the opposite outside strand and cross it over the new middle strand. Continue this pattern until you get to the ends of the strands, then pinch the tips together to seal. Rotate the loaf so the unbraided side is facing you, then repeat the pattern on that end.

To shape a 4-braid loaf, connect 4 strands of equal weight and length at one end, spreading the other ends out with the tips facing you. From the left, number the strands 1, 2, 3, 4. Follow this pattern: 4 over 2, 1 over 3, and 2 over 3. Repeat until you get to the ends of the strands, then pinch the tips together to seal.

continued

To shape a 5-braid loaf, connect 5 strands of equal weight and length at one end, spreading the other ends out with the tips facing you. From the left, number the strands 1, 2, 3, 4, 5. Follow this pattern: 1 over 3, 2 over 3, and 5 over 2. Repeat until you get to the ends of the strands, then pinch the tips together to seal.

To shape a 6-braid loaf, connect 6 strands of equal weight and length at one end, spreading the other ends out with the tips facing you. From the left, number the strands 1 through 6 and bring strand 6 over strand 1 to build up the end of the loaf. Strand 5 has now become the new strand 6, and the old strand 6 is now strand 1. Now follow this pattern: 2 over 6, 1 over 3, 5 over 1, and 6 over 4. Repeat the pattern until you get to the ends of the strands, then pinch the tips together to seal.

Hoagie and Cheesesteak Rolls

MAKES 10 SEVEN-INCH ROLLS OR 5 FOOT-LONG ROLLS

I get emails all the time asking for Philadelphia-style hoagie and cheesesteak rolls. There is something about the cultural connection we Philly folk have with these iconic sandwiches that makes many people believe that Philadelphia's Amoroso's Baking Company is the only place to find a good hoagie roll, which is, of course, not true. The key to this type of roll is a nice balance of texture and flavor, somewhere between lean dough and soft enriched dough, with just enough "chew" to stand up to the fillings without making it overly hard to eat the darn thing. The overnight fermentation method is ideal for this because it brings out maximum flavor with very little hands-on time. The optional barley malt syrup provides a nice undertone of flavor that's difficult to identify and also helps with crust color. This dough also makes great Kaiser rolls.

$5^1/_3$ cups (24 oz / 680 g) unbleached bread flour

2 teaspoons (0.5 oz / 14 g) salt, or 1 tablespoon coarse kosher salt

1 tablespoon (0.5 oz / 14 g) sugar

$1^1/_2$ teaspoons (0.5 oz / 14 g) barley malt syrup, or $^3/_4$ teaspoon (0.17 oz / 5 g) diastatic malt powder (optional)

1 egg (1.75 oz / 50 g)

3 tablespoons (1.5 oz / 43 g) vegetable oil

1 cup (8 oz / 227 g) lukewarm water (about 95°F or 35°C)

$^1/_2$ cup plus 2 tablespoons (5 oz / 142 g) lukewarm milk (any kind; at about 95°F or 35°C)

$2^1/_4$ teaspoons (0.25 oz / 7 g) instant yeast

DO AHEAD

In a mixing bowl, whisk the flour, salt, and sugar together. In a separate bowl, whisk the malt syrup, egg, and oil together. Separately, combine the water and milk, then whisk in the instant yeast until dissolved.

Add the oil mixture and the water mixture to the dry ingredients. If using a mixer, switch to the dough hook and mix on the lowest speed, or continue mixing by hand, for 4 minutes to form a coarse ball of dough. Let the dough rest for 5 minutes.

Mix for 2 minutes more on medium-low speed or by hand with a spoon, adjusting with flour or water as needed to form a smooth, supple, and tacky but not sticky dough.

Transfer the dough to a lightly floured work surface and knead for 1 minute, working in more flour or water as needed. Form the dough into a ball.

Place the dough in a clean, lightly oiled bowl large enough to hold the dough when it doubles in size. Cover the bowl tightly with plastic wrap, then immediately put it in the refrigerator overnight or for up to 4 days. (If you plan to bake the dough in batches over different days, you can portion the dough and place it into two or more oiled bowls at this stage.)

ON BAKING DAY

Remove the dough from the refrigerator about 2 hours before you plan to bake and transfer it to a lightly floured work surface. Divide the cold dough into 4-ounce (113 g) pieces for 7-inch rolls or 8-ounce (227 g) pieces for foot-long rolls. Flatten each piece of dough with your hand, then form it into a 4-inch torpedo shape, or a 7-inch torpedo shape for foot-long rolls, much as you would a *bâtard* (see page 21). Let each piece of dough rest as you move on to the other pieces. When you return to the first torpedo, gently roll it back and forth to extend it out to about 7 inches, or 13 inches for a foot-long roll. The roll should have only a very slight taper at the ends. Place the rolls on a sheet pan lined with parchment paper or a silicone mat with about 2 inches between the rolls (it may take 2 pans if you bake the entire batch). The rolls may shrink back about 1 inch as you pan them. Mist the tops of the rolls with spray oil, cover loosely with plastic wrap, then let the dough rise at room temperature for about 1 hour.

Remove the plastic wrap from the rolls. Continue to proof the dough for another 15 minutes, uncovered. The dough will rise only slightly—not more than $1^1/_2$ times its original size.

Use a sharp serrated knife or razor blade to cut a slit down the center of each roll, about $^1/_4$ inch deep and about $3^1/_2$ inches long (or 8 inches for foot-long rolls). Let the dough proof for 15 minutes after you make the cuts. Place a steam pan in the oven (a cast-iron frying pan or sheet pan works just fine) and preheat the oven to 425°F (218°C).

Transfer the rolls to the oven, pour 1 cup of hot water into the steam pan, then lower the oven temperature to 400°F (204°C).

Bake for 10 minutes, then rotate the pan and bake for another 10 to 20 minutes, until the rolls are a light golden brown and their internal temperature is 190°F (88°C) in the center.

Cool on a wire rack for at least 1 hour before slicing or serving.

VARIATION

Feel free to substitute whole wheat flour or other whole grain flours for some of the bread flour. If you do so, increase the water by about 1 tablespoon (0.5 oz / 14 g) for every 7 tablespoons (2 oz / 56.5 g) of whole grain flour you substitute.

Many-Seed Bread

MAKES 2 LARGE LOAVES OR MANY ROLLS

I enjoy seeds in bread. They add all sorts of valuable nutrients, and they just taste so good. This bread is similar to a classic German *Mehrkorn* bread, loaded with seeds and just a touch of whole wheat flour (though you can certainly use more whole wheat if you like). I love to make sandwiches with it, especially peanut butter and jelly, to toast it, or to simply eat it by the slice. Take my word for it, it tastes really good.

Only the sunflower and pumpkin seeds need to be toasted; the sesame and flaxseeds can go in without toasting. Natural sesame seeds, which are light brown because they still have their hulls, are much more appealing in this bread than white sesame seeds, which have had the hulls polished off. If you're feeling adventurous, you can use other combinations of seeds. Try adding lightly toasted chopped walnuts or pecans. Because the dough will stiffen overnight in the refrigerator as the seeds slowly absorb moisture, it's important to have a very soft, supple dough—even a tad sticky—before you put it away for the night.

5 cups (22.5 oz / 638 g) unbleached bread flour

$^2/_3$ cup (3 oz / 85 g) whole wheat or whole rye flour

$^1/_2$ cup (2 oz / 56.5 g) sesame seeds

$^1/_3$ cup (1 oz / 28.5 g) sunflower seeds, lightly toasted

$^1/_3$ cup (1 oz / 28.5 g) pumpkin seeds, lightly toasted

3 tablespoons (1 oz / 28.5 g) flaxseeds

$2^1/_4$ teaspoons (0.6 oz / 17 g) salt, or $3^1/_2$ teaspoons coarse kosher salt

$1^1/_2$ tablespoons (0.5 oz / 14 g) instant yeast

3 tablespoons (2 oz / 56.5 g) honey or agave nectar,
or $^1/_4$ cup brown sugar

$1^1/_2$ cups (12 oz / 340 g) lukewarm water (about 95°F or 35°C)

$^3/_4$ cup (6 oz / 170 g) lukewarm buttermilk, any other milk,
or yogurt (about 95°F or 35°C)

Sesame seeds or poppy seeds, for garnish (optional)

DO AHEAD

Combine the flours, seeds, salt, yeast, honey, water, and buttermilk in a mixing bowl. If using a mixer, use the paddle attachment and mix on the lowest speed for 2 minutes. If mixing by hand, stir with a large spoon. The dough should be sticky, coarse, and shaggy. Let the dough rest for 5 minutes.

Switch to the dough hook and mix on medium-low speed, or continue mixing by hand, for 3 to 4 minutes, adding flour only as needed to keep the dough ball together, but making sure the dough remains soft and very tacky or slightly sticky. (In the unlikely event that the dough is too stiff, work in a little more water.)

Transfer the dough to a floured work surface. Lightly knead it by hand for about 3 minutes, adding more flour as needed to prevent sticking. The dough will still be soft and slightly sticky but should hold together to form a soft, supple ball.

Place the dough in a clean, lightly oiled bowl, cover the bowl tightly with plastic wrap, and refrigerate overnight or for up to 4 days. (If you plan to bake the dough in batches over different days, you can portion the dough and place it into two or more oiled bowls at this stage.)

ON BAKING DAY

Remove the dough from the refrigerator about 2 hours before you plan to bake. Shape the cold dough into one or more sandwich loaves (see page 23), using 28 ounces (794 g) of dough for $4^1/_2$ by 8-inch loaf pans and 36 ounces (1.02 kg) of dough for 5 by 9-inch pans; into freestanding loaves of any size, which you can shape as *bâtards* (see page 21), baguettes (see page 22), or *boules* (see page 20); or into rolls (see page 25), using about 2 ounces (56.5 g) of dough per roll. When shaping, use only as much flour on the work surface as necessary to keep the dough from sticking. **For sandwich loaves,** proof the dough in greased loaf pans. **For freestanding loaves and rolls,** line a sheet pan with parchment paper or a silicone mat and proof the dough on the pan.

Brush the top of the shaped dough with water and sprinkle with sesame seeds or poppy seeds. (For a shinier crust and better sticking of the seeds, you could brush with egg white wash instead of water; see page 135). Mist with spray oil and cover loosely with plastic wrap. Let the dough rise at room temperature for $1^1/_2$ to 2 hours, until increased to about $1^1/_2$ times its original size. In loaf pans, the dough should dome at least 1 inch above the rim.

About 15 minutes before baking, preheat the oven to 350°F (177°C), or 300°F (149°C) for a convection oven.

Bake loaves for 20 minutes, then rotate the pan; rotate rolls after 8 minutes. The total baking time is 45 to 55 minutes for loaves, and only 20 to 25 minutes for rolls. The bread is done when it has a rich golden color, the loaf sounds hollow when thumped on the bottom, and the internal temperature is above 185°F (85°C) in the center.

Cool on a wire rack for at least 20 minutes for rolls and 1 hour for large loaves before slicing or serving.

Soft Sandwich Bread and Rolls

This type of dough is often referred to as milk dough, since the primary enrichment is milk, whether whole, skim, buttermilk, or powdered. It also contains a fair amount of sweetener and some form of fat or oil. All of these enrichments serve to keep the bread soft and slightly sweet. Because of the many enrichments, the dough has a larger percentage of yeast than lean dough, so it's especially important to put it into the refrigerator right after it's mixed to avoid overfermentation. If you use honey or agave nectar instead of sugar, increase the amount of flour by $3^1/_2$ to 7 tablespoons (1 to 2 oz / 28.5 to 56.5 g). This dough makes wonderful sandwich bread and can also be used to make many different types of rolls, including hamburger and hot dog buns. See the variations on page 106 for a variety of possibilities.

1 tablespoon (0.33 oz / 9 g) instant yeast

$1^3/_4$ cups plus 2 tablespoons (15 oz / 425 g) lukewarm milk
(any kind; at about 95°F or 35°C)

$6^1/_4$ cups (28 oz / 794 g) unbleached bread flour

2 teaspoons (0.5 oz / 14 g) salt, or 1 tablespoon coarse kosher salt

$5^1/_2$ tablespoons (2.75 oz / 78 g) sugar, or $^1/_4$ cup honey or agave nectar

6 tablespoons (3 oz / 85 g) vegetable oil or melted unsalted butter

1 egg (1.75 oz / 50 g)

DO AHEAD

Whisk the yeast into the lukewarm milk until dissolved. Set aside for 1 to 5 minutes.

Combine the flour, salt, sugar, oil, and egg in a mixing bowl, then pour in the milk mixture. If using a mixer, use the paddle attachment and mix on the lowest speed for 2 minutes. If mixing by hand, use a large spoon and stir for about 2 minutes. The dough should be coarse and slightly sticky.

Switch to the dough hook and mix on medium-low speed for 4 to 5 minutes, or knead by hand on a lightly floured work surface for 4 to 5 minutes, until the dough is soft, supple, and tacky but not sticky.

Whichever mixing method you use, knead the dough by hand for 1 minute, then form it into a ball.

continued, page 108

Making Rolls

You can use this dough to make any number of soft rolls (see page 25 for shaping instructions), such as **silver dollars** (about 1 ounce each), **butterflake** (about 1$\frac{1}{2}$ to 2 ounces each), **hot dog and hamburger buns** (about 2$\frac{1}{2}$ to 3$\frac{1}{2}$ ounces each), and various **knotted rolls** (about 1$\frac{1}{2}$ ounces to 3 ounces each).

Soft rolls should be brushed with egg wash (see page 135) a few minutes before baking. After applying the egg wash, you can garnish with poppy seeds or sesame seeds if you like. The total baking time is 12 to 18 minutes, depending on size, at 400°F (204°C).

To make butterflake rolls, roll the dough to a $\frac{1}{4}$ inch thick rectangle or oval. Brush the surface of the dough with melted butter. Use a pizza cutter to cut the dough into four even strips, then stack the strips neatly on top of each other. Use a metal pastry scraper to cut the stacked strips into 1 inch wide units (about 1$\frac{1}{2}$ to 2 ounces each). Place the small stacks on their sides in an oiled muffin pan. Proof and bake following the recipe.

Place the dough in a clean, lightly oiled bowl, cover the bowl tightly with plastic wrap, and refrigerate overnight or for up to 4 days. (If you plan to bake the dough in batches over different days, you can portion the dough and place it into two or more oiled bowls at this stage.)

ON BAKING DAY

Remove the dough from the refrigerator about $2^1/_2$ hours before you plan to bake and divide it in half; each piece should weigh about 25 ounces (709 g), which is perfect for $4^1/_2$ by 8-inch pans. For a 5 by 9-inch pan, use 28 to 32 ounces (794 to 907 g) of dough. Shape into sandwich loaves (see page 23), then place them in greased loaf pans to rise. (You can also make a variety of different rolls using the guidelines on page 106.) Mist the dough with spray oil and cover the pans loosely with plastic wrap; then let the dough rise at room temperature for about $2^1/_2$ hours, until it domes about 1 inch above the rims of the pans.

About 15 minutes before baking, preheat the oven to 350°F (177°C).

Bake for 20 minutes, then rotate the pans and bake for another 20 to 30 minutes. The bread is done when the top is golden brown, the sides are firm and brown, the loaf sounds hollow when thumped on the bottom, and the internal temperature is at least 185°F (85°C) in the center.

Remove from the pans and cool on a wire rack for at least 1 hour before slicing or serving.

Soft Rye Sandwich Bread

There are many ways to make rye bread, and every bread lover has a favorite version. But when push comes to shove, the style that sells the most is soft sandwich rye. This version includes the optional use of cocoa powder, which darkens the bread in the style of pumpernickel. Other optional ingredients, whether caraway, minced dried onion, or nigella seeds (also known as black onion seeds), transform this recipe into various regional favorites. Adding orange oil or extract and anise seeds, for example, turns it into a Swedish-style *limpa* rye bread.

You can use various types of rye flour in this recipe. The version most commonly sold is the "white flour" version of rye, with the bran and germ sifted out. But if you look around, you should be able to find stone-ground, whole grain, or dark rye flour, as well as pumpernickel flour. You could even use rye chops or rye meal, which are more coarsely ground, resembling cracked wheat or steel-cut oats. The trade-off is that whole rye flour is more healthful, while light rye yields a softer, lighter loaf. The choice is yours. The molasses is an important flavor component in this bread, but feel free to reduce the amount or replace it with sorghum syrup or golden sugar syrup. Just don't use blackstrap molasses, which is too strong; look for a product labeled "old-fashioned," "fancy," or "unsulfured."

SOUR RYE STARTER

1/4 cup (2 oz / 56.5 g) mother starter (page 42), cold or at room temperature

1²/3 cups (7.5 oz / 213 g) rye flour

3/4 cup (6 oz / 170 g) water, at room temperature

DOUGH

All of the sour rye starter (15.5 oz / 439.5 g)

1¹/2 cups plus 3 tablespoons (13.5 oz / 383 g) lukewarm water (about 95°F or 35°C)

1¹/2 tablespoons (1 oz / 28.5 g) molasses

1/4 cup (2 oz / 56.5 g) vegetable oil

2¹/4 teaspoons (0.25 oz / 7 g) instant yeast

5¹/3 cups (24 oz / 680 g) unbleached bread flour

continued

3 tablespoons (1 oz / 28.5 g) cocoa powder (optional)

2³/₈ teaspoons (0.6 oz / 17 g) salt, or 3¹/₂ teaspoons coarse kosher salt

1 tablespoon caraway seeds, nigella seeds, minced dried onion, or anise seeds (optional)

³/₄ teaspoon (0.17 oz / 5 g) orange oil or 1 tablespoon (0.5 oz / 14 g) orange extract (optional)

1 egg white, for egg wash (optional)

1 tablespoon water, for egg wash (optional)

DO AHEAD

To make the starter, combine all of the ingredients in a mixing bowl. If using a mixer, use the paddle attachment and mix on the lowest speed for 1 minute, then increase to medium speed for about 30 seconds. If mixing by hand, stir for about 2 minutes, until well blended. The starter should feel tacky or slightly sticky; if you use coarse rye flour, it will feel like modeling clay, and you may need to add another 2 tablespoons (1 oz / 28.5 g) of water to make it pliable.

Transfer the starter to a clean, lightly oiled bowl, cover the bowl loosely, and leave it at room temperature for 6 to 8 hours, until the starter swells noticeably in size and develops a tangy aroma. If you plan to use the starter the same day, allow 1 more hour of fermentation. Otherwise, put the starter in the refrigerator for up to 4 days.

To make the dough, cut the starter into 10 to 12 pieces and put them in a mixing bowl. Separately, combine the water, molasses, and vegetable oil, then whisk in the yeast until dissolved. Let stand for 1 minute, then pour the mixture over the starter and mix with the paddle attachment on the lowest speed or with a large spoon for about 1 minute to soften the starter.

Add the flour, cocoa powder, salt, and seeds and orange oil. Switch to the dough hook and mix on the lowest speed, or continue mixing by hand, for 4 minutes. If the dough rides up on the dough hook, stop the mixer and scrape it back into the bowl. The dough should form a coarse ball that's soft, supple, and very tacky, verging on sticky. Let the dough rest for 5 minutes.

Mix on medium-low speed or by hand for 2 minutes more, adding flour or water as needed to make a smooth, supple, tacky ball of dough.

Transfer the dough to a lightly floured work surface and knead by hand for about 20 seconds, working in any final adjustments with flour or water, then form the dough into a ball.

Place the dough in a clean, lightly oiled bowl, cover the bowl with plastic wrap, and immediately place it in the refrigerator overnight or for up to 4 days. (If you plan to bake the dough

continued, page 112

Multicolor Rye Loaves

To make marbled rye bread, make two batches of dough, one light and one dark.

To shape marbled rye loaves, cut each dough into 12 even-size pieces. Separate the pieces into 2 piles, with an equal number of dark and light pieces in each. Form each of the piles into a solid mass of dough by pressing them together. Shape each into a *bâtard*, as shown on page 21. You can bake the loaves freestanding (which is what I recommend) or in greased 4^1/$_2$ by 8^1/$_2$-inch loaf pans. For freestanding loaves, transfer to parchment-lined baking sheets (1 per loaf). Cover and proof.

For braided marbled rye, divide the light and dark doughs into 4 even-size pieces each. Roll each piece into a strand 10 to 12 inches in length, thicker in the middle and slightly tapered toward the ends. Braid 2 light and 2 dark pieces together using the 4-braid method shown on page 98. You can bake the loaves freestanding (which is what I recommend) or in greased 4^1/$_2$ by 8^1/$_2$-inch loaf pans. For freestanding loaves, transfer to parchment-lined baking sheets (1 per loaf). Cover and proof.

For bull's-eye loaves, divide the light and dark doughs into 4 even-size pieces each. Use a rolling pin to roll each piece into an oblong about 5 inches wide and 8 inches long. Roll up a dark rye piece and shape it into a *bâtard* about 8 inches long, as shown on page 21. Take a light rye piece and wrap it around the *bâtard*, then seal the seam. Repeat with the remaining dough to make 4 small loaves. Place the loaves on 2 parchment-lined sheet pans, seam side down, then cover and proof.

For spiral loaves, divide the light and dark doughs into 4 even-size pieces each. Use a rolling pin to roll each piece into an oblong about 5 inches wide and 8 inches long. Take a light rye piece and lay a dark rye piece on top, then add another light rye piece and another dark rye piece. Roll this stack up and shape it into a *bâtard*, as shown on page 21, and seal the seam. Repeat with the remaining dough to make 2 loaves. Place the loaves on 2 parchment-lined sheet pans or in 2 greased 4^1/$_2$ by 8^1/$_2$-inch loaf pans, seam side down, then cover and proof.

in batches over different days, you can portion the dough and place it into two or more oiled bowls at this stage.) If baking the bread on the same day, leave the dough at room temperature for 90 minutes to 2 hours, until it doubles in size, and then proceed to shaping. The final rising time, after shaping, will be 60 to 90 minutes.

ON BAKING DAY

Remove the dough from the refrigerator about 3 hours before you plan to bake. Shape the dough into one or more sandwich loaves (see page 23), using 28 ounces (794 g) of dough for $4^1/_2$ by 8-inch loaf pans and 36 ounces (1.02 kg) of dough for 5 by 9-inch pans; or shape it into freestanding loaves of any size, which you can shape as *bâtards* (see page 21), baguettes (see page 22), or *boules* (see page 20). **For sandwich loaves,** proof the dough in greased loaf pans. **For freestanding loaves,** line a sheet pan with parchment paper or a silicone mat and proof the dough on the pan. Mist the dough with spray oil and cover loosely with plastic wrap, then let the dough rise at room temperature for about $2^1/_2$ to 3 hours, until increased to about $1^1/_2$ times its original size. In loaf pans, the dough should dome at least 1 inch above the rim.

About 15 minutes before baking, preheat the oven to 350°F (177°C) for sandwich loaves or 400°F (204°C) for freestanding loaves. If you'd like to use an egg wash to make the crust more shiny, whisk the egg white and water together, then brush the mixture over the tops of the loaves. Scoring is optional and only recommended for freestanding loaves. If you'd like to score them, do so just prior to baking, making 3 to 5 horizontal cuts across the top, about $1/_2$ inch deep.

Bake for 20 minutes, then rotate the pans and bake for another 20 to 35 minutes, depending on the size of the loaves. The total baking time is 40 to 55 minutes for large sandwich loaves and 25 to 45 minutes for freestanding loaves, depending on size. The bread is done when the loaves sound hollow when thumped on the bottom and the internal temperature is about 190°F (88°C).

Remove the loaves from the pans and cool on a wire rack for at least 1 hour before slicing or serving.

VARIATION

Like most bakery rye breads, this recipe calls for sourdough starter, which actually contains all of the rye flour. If you don't have a mother starter, you can replace the sour rye starter by adding all of the rye flour from the starter instructions to the final dough, along with 6 to 7 ounces (170 to 198 g) of buttermilk or yogurt to provide some acidic tang.

Wild Rice and Onion Bread

MAKES 2 LARGE LOAVES OR MANY ROLLS

After *struan*, wild rice and onion bread was the most popular bread at Brother Juniper's Bakery, and a version of this recipe appears in my first book, *Brother Juniper's Bread Book*. The recipe calls for wild rice, but it can also be made with brown rice or a combination of wild and brown rice, or any other cooked grain. At Brother Juniper's, during the holiday season we even added parsley, sage, rosemary, thyme, garlic powder, and black pepper, which made for a wonderful bread for stuffing turkey. Note that it only takes about 1/4 cup of uncooked wild rice to make 1 cup (6 oz, by weight) of cooked wild rice; still, if you're going to cook wild rice especially for this recipe, you might as well make a bigger batch and freeze 1-cup packets for future use—or have it with dinner!

This new version uses the overnight fermentation method. The yeast is added directly to the bowl, not rehydrated with the warm water and buttermilk. You can use either dried or fresh onions, and you can form the loaves into any size or shape. Dried onions are about one-tenth the weight of fresh onions and will absorb water from the dough, while fresh onions will leach moisture back into the dough. If you use dried onions, don't rehydrate them before adding them to the dough, but do be aware that you may have to add an extra 2 to 4 tablespoons (1 to 2 oz) of water while mixing.

6 cups (27 oz / 765 g) unbleached bread flour

2 1/4 teaspoons (0.6 oz / 17 g) salt, or 3 1/2 teaspoons coarse kosher salt

2 tablespoons (0.66 oz / 19 g) instant yeast

1 cup (6 oz / 170 g) cooked wild rice or another cooked grain

1/4 cup (2 oz / 56.5 g) brown sugar

1 1/2 cups (12 oz / 340 g) lukewarm water (about 95°F or 35°C)

1/2 cup (4 oz / 113 g) lukewarm buttermilk or any other milk (about 95°F or 35°C)

1/4 cup (1 oz / 28.5 g) minced or chopped dried onions, or 2 cups (8 oz / 227 g) diced fresh onion (about 1 large onion)

1 egg white, for egg wash (optional)

1 tablespoon water, for egg wash (optional)

Combine all of the ingredients, except the egg wash, in a mixing bowl. If using a mixer, use the paddle attachment and mix on the lowest speed for 1 minute. If mixing by hand, use a large spoon and stir for 1 minute. The dough should be sticky, coarse, and shaggy. Let the dough rest for 5 minutes.

Switch to the dough hook and mix on medium-low speed, or continue mixing by hand, for 4 minutes, adjusting with flour or water as needed to keep the dough ball together. The dough should be soft, supple, and slightly sticky.

Transfer the dough to a lightly floured work surface. Knead the dough for 2 to 3 minutes, adding more flour as needed to prevent sticking. The dough will still be soft and slightly sticky but will hold together to form a soft, supple ball. Place the dough in a clean, lightly oiled bowl, cover the bowl tightly with plastic wrap, and immediately refrigerate overnight or for up to 4 days. (If you plan to bake the dough in batches over different days, you can portion the dough and place it into two or more oiled bowls at this stage.)

ON BAKING DAY

Remove the dough from the refrigerator about 2 hours before you plan to bake. Shape the dough into one or more sandwich loaves (see page 23), using 28 ounces (794 g) of dough for 4$^1/_2$ by 8-inch loaf pans and 36 ounces (1.02 kg) of dough for 5 by 9-inch pans; into freestanding loaves of any size, which you can shape as *bâtards* (see page 21), baguettes (see page 22), or *boules* (see page 20); or into rolls (see page 25), using 2 ounces (56.5 g) of dough per roll. When shaping, use only as much flour as necessary to keep the dough from sticking. For sandwich loaves, proof the dough in greased loaf pans. For freestanding loaves and rolls, line a sheet pan with parchment paper or a silicone mat and proof the dough on the pan.

Mist the top of the dough with spray oil and cover loosely with plastic wrap. Let the dough rise at room temperature for 1$^1/_2$ to 2 hours, until increased to about 1$^1/_2$ times its original size. In loaf pans, the dough should dome at least 1 inch above the rim. If you'd like to make the rolls more shiny, whisk the egg white and water together, brush the tops of the rolls with the egg wash (see page 135) just before they're ready to bake.

About 15 minutes before baking, preheat the oven to 350°F (177°C), or 300°F (149°C) for a convection oven.

Bake the loaves for 10 to 15 minutes, then rotate the pan; rotate rolls after 8 minutes. The total baking time is 45 to 55 minutes for loaves, and only 20 to 25 minutes for rolls. The bread is done when it has a rich golden color, the loaf sounds hollow when thumped on the bottom, and the internal temperature is above 185°F (85°C) in the center.

Cool on a wire rack for at least 20 minutes for rolls or 1 hour for loaves before slicing.

SOFT AND CRUSTY CHEESE BREADS

Not everyone knows that before I was a bread baker I was a cheese maker, and in both pursuits I've been fascinated by the transformational aspect, in which a basic ingredient becomes something new and wonderful—how wheat becomes bread, and milk becomes another fascinating and mysterious foodstuff. I never tire of cheese in any of its hundreds (maybe thousands) of forms. And together, bread and cheese always make a winning, almost magical combination that's found in many beloved forms throughout the world, including pizza, quesadillas, focaccia, and grilled cheese sandwiches, not to mention cheese fondue. There are a number of ways to incorporate cheese into bread, and I've tried most of them. In my opinion, it's a waste to add grated cheese to dough and mix it in. While this does create a soft texture and a tastier loaf, the subtle nuances of the cheese's flavor are completely eclipsed by the dough, and the cheese seems to disappear. I prefer to roll cheese in during the shaping stage.

The types of cheese that can be used are endless, though I do advise against using dry, hard cheese exclusively, as it tends to disappear into the bread and burn when exposed to the surface heat. Choose a good melting cheese or use a mixture of soft melting cheeses and intense, dry cheeses. As for wet cheeses like blue, feta, and brie, I say, why not? You don't always have to use expensive cheese, either; supermarket brand Cheddar, Swiss, or Mozzarella will work just fine. The main rule of thumb is to use enough cheese that it makes its presence known. If you're going to put cheese in bread, you don't want it to disappear into the background. Once you've learned how to incorporate cheese into bread using the next two recipes, you can use the same technique with many other recipes in this book, especially the basic lean bread and some of the rich holiday breads. (Brioche with cured meat and cheese baked into it is one of the wonders of the world.)

Soft Cheese Bread

MAKES 2 LARGE LOAVES OR MANY ROLLS

You can use any kind of beer in this recipe, as both light and dark brews add subtle flavors that will complement the cheese.

6¼ cups (28 oz / 794 g) unbleached bread flour

2 teaspoons (0.5 oz / 14 g) salt, or 1 tablespoon coarse kosher salt

5 tablespoons (2.25 oz / 64 g) granulated or brown sugar,
or 3½ tablespoons honey or agave nectar

1 cup (8 oz / 227 g) lukewarm water or beer (about 95°F or 35°C)

1 cup plus 2 tablespoons (9 oz / 255 g) lukewarm buttermilk
or any other milk (about 95°F or 35°C)

1½ tablespoons (0.5 oz / 14 g) instant yeast

¼ cup (2 oz / 56.5 g) melted unsalted butter or vegetable oil

1¾ cups (7 oz / 198 g) diced onion (about 1 medium onion)
or 1 small bunch of fresh chives (1 oz / 28.5 g), minced (optional)

2½ cups (12 oz / 340 g) grated, shredded, or cubed cheese

DO AHEAD

In a mixing bowl, whisk the flour, salt, and sugar together (if using honey or agave nectar, dissolve it in the lukewarm water instead). Separately, combine the water and buttermilk, whisk in the yeast until dissolved, then pour the mixture and the melted butter into the dry ingredients. If using a mixer, use the paddle attachment and mix on the lowest speed for 2 minutes. If mixing by hand, use a large spoon and stir for about 2 minutes. Let the dough rest for 5 minutes.

Switch to the dough hook and mix on medium-low speed, or continue mixing by hand, for 3 minutes, adjusting with flour or liquid as needed. The dough should be soft, supple, and tacky but not sticky. Add the onions and mix on the lowest speed or continue mixing by hand for 1 minute, until the onions are evenly distributed.

Transfer the dough to a lightly floured work surface and knead for 1 or 2 minutes to make any final adjustments, then form the dough into a ball.

Place the dough in a clean, lightly oiled bowl, cover the bowl with plastic wrap, and immediately refrigerate overnight or for up to 4 days. (If you plan to bake the dough in batches over

different days, you can portion the dough and place it into two or more oiled bowls at this stage.) The dough should double in size in the refrigerator. If you want to bake the bread the same day you mix the dough, don't refrigerate the final dough; just let it rest at room temperature for 60 to 90 minutes, until it doubles in size. Then proceed to shaping and baking as described below.

ON BAKING DAY

Remove the dough from the refrigerator about 2 hours before you plan to bake. Transfer the dough to a lightly floured work surface and divide it into 2 equal pieces, each weighing about 2 pounds (907 g). Dust each piece with flour, then use a rolling pin to roll them into rectangles about 8 inches wide and 12 inches high. Spread half of the cheese over the surface of one rectangle and roll the dough up like a rug, from the bottom to the top, to form a log. If any cheese falls out, tuck it back in or save it for the second loaf. Seal the seam with your fingertips. **For a sandwich loaf,** proof in a greased $4^{1}/_{2}$ by 8-inch loaf pan (or a 5 by 9-inch pan if using onions, which increase the volume of the dough). **For a freestanding bâtard or rolls** (see page 21), proof on a sheet pan lined with parchment paper or a silicone mat. Another option is to cut the log into $1^{1}/_{2}$-inch slices to make spiral rolls; place spiral rolls about 1 inch apart in greased round pans or on a parchment-lined sheet pan. Mist the shaped dough with spray oil and cover loosely with plastic wrap, then let the dough rise at room temperature for about 90 minutes, until increased to about $1^{1}/_{2}$ times its original size. In loaf pans, the dough should dome about 1 inch above the rim.

About 15 minutes before baking, preheat the oven to 350°F (177°C), or 300°F (149°C) for a convection oven. Because of the cheese, there may be air pockets or tunnels in the risen dough that could cause it to separate in the spirals (cubed cheese creates fewer air pockets than grated or shredded cheese). To minimize this, poke through the top crust in a few spots with a skewer or toothpick. The dough may fall a bit, but it will recover in the oven.

Bake loaves for 20 minutes, then rotate the pans; rotate rolls after 10 minutes. The total baking time is about 50 minutes for loaves, and only 20 to 25 minutes for rolls. The bread is done when it's a deep golden brown and the internal temperature is above 185°F (85°C) in the center.

Remove from the pans and cool on a wire rack for at least 15 minutes for rolls and about 1 hour for loaves before slicing or serving.

You can substitute potato water (leftover from boiling potatoes) for the water or beer, which will make the dough even softer. The milk provides some tenderness and color, but if you prefer a leaner bread you can replace it with an equal amount of water or potato water.

Feel free to replace some of the bread flour with an equivalent amount (by weight) of whole wheat flour or rye flour. If you do so, increase the amount of water by about 1 tablespoon (0.5 oz / 14 g) for every 7 tablespoons (1 oz / 28.5 g) of whole grain flour you use.

If you would like to avoid the air pockets caused by the melting cheese, you can knead cubed cheese into the dough after the overnight rise, just before shaping, rather than rolling it up in the dough. This will create little cheese bursts throughout the loaf instead of a spiral.

Crusty Cheese Bread

MAKES 2 LARGE LOAVES OR 3 SMALLER LOAVES

Because the cheese may bubble and run out of this bread while in the oven, I advise baking the loaves on a parchment-lined sheet pan rather than directly on a baking stone. Any cheese that does run out onto the pan will be like a crispy little cheese snack, so it won't go to waste.

SOURDOUGH STARTER

$^1/_4$ cup (2 oz / 56.5 g) mother starter (page 42), cold or at room temperature

$1^1/_3$ cups (6 oz / 170 g) unbleached bread flour

$^1/_2$ cup (4 oz / 113 g) water

DOUGH

All of the sourdough starter (12 oz / 340 g)

1 cup (8 oz / 227 g) lukewarm water or potato water (about 95°F or 35°C)

$^1/_2$ cup (4 oz / 113 g) lukewarm whole or low-fat milk (about 95°F or 35°C)

$2^1/_4$ teaspoons (0.25 oz / 7 g) instant yeast

$1^1/_2$ tablespoons (1 oz / 28.5 g) honey or agave nectar

$4^1/_2$ cups (20 oz / 567 g) unbleached bread flour

continued

2 teaspoons (0.5 oz / 14 g) salt, or 1 tablespoon coarse kosher salt

1³/₄ cups (7 oz / 198 g) diced onion (about 1 medium onion)
or 1 small bunch of fresh chives (1 oz / 28.5 g), minced (optional)

2¹/₂ cups (12 oz / 340 g) grated, shredded, or cubed cheese

DO AHEAD

To make the starter, combine all of the ingredients in a mixing bowl. If using a mixer, use the paddle attachment and mix on the lowest speed for 1 minute, then increase to medium speed for about 30 seconds. If mixing by hand, stir for about 2 minutes, until well blended. The starter should feel doughlike and tacky or slightly sticky; if not, stir in additional flour or water as needed.

Transfer the starter to a lightly floured work surface and knead for about 30 seconds. Place the starter in a clean, lightly oiled bowl, cover the bowl loosely, and leave at room temperature for 6 to 8 hours, until the starter increases to about 1¹/₂ times its original size. If you plan to use the starter the same day, allow 1 more hour of fermentation so that it nearly doubles in size. Otherwise, put the starter in the refrigerator for up to 4 days.

To make the dough, chop the starter into 10 to 12 pieces and put them in a mixing bowl. Separately, combine the water and milk, then add the yeast and honey and whisk until dissolved. Pour the mixture over the starter and stir to soften the starter.

Add the flour and salt. If using a mixer, use the dough hook and mix on the lowest speed for about 4 minutes. If mixing by hand, stir with a large spoon for about 4 minutes. The dough should be soft, supple, and tacky but not sticky. Let the dough rest for 5 minutes.

Mix with the dough hook on medium-low speed, or continue to mix by hand, for another 3 minutes, adding flour or liquid as needed to maintain a soft, supple, and tacky but not sticky dough. Add the onions and mix on the lowest speed or continue mixing by hand for another minute, until the onions are evenly distributed.

Transfer the dough to a lightly floured work surface and knead for 1 or 2 minutes to make any final adjustments, then form the dough into a ball.

Place the dough in a clean, lightly oiled bowl, cover the bowl with plastic wrap, and immediately refrigerate overnight or for up to 4 days. (If you plan to bake the dough in batches over different days, you can portion the dough and place it into two or more oiled bowls at this stage.) The dough should double in size in the refrigerator. If you want to bake the bread the same day you mix the dough, don't refrigerate the final dough; just let it rest at room temperature for about 60 to 90 minutes, until it doubles in size. Then proceed to shaping and baking, as described below.

Remove the dough from the refrigerator about 2 hours before you plan to bake. Transfer the dough to a lightly floured work surface and divide it into 2 equal pieces, each weighing about 2 pounds (907 g). Dust each piece with flour, then use your hands to gently press them into rectangles 8 inches wide and 12 inches deep. Spread half of the cheese over the surface of one rectangle and roll the dough up like a rug, from the bottom to the top, to form a log. If any cheese falls out, tuck it back in or save it for the second loaf. Seal the seam with your fingertips. Shape the log into a *bâtard* (see page 21) or extend it into a baguette-style loaf (see page 22) by gently rocking the loaf back and forth. Place the loaves on parchment-lined sheet pans, mist with spray oil, and cover loosely with plastic wrap. Let the dough rise at room temperature for 90 minutes to 2 hours, until the loaves begin to noticeably swell in size.

About 45 minutes before baking, preheat the oven to 450°F (232°C) and prepare it for hearth baking (see page 30). About 15 minutes before baking, uncover the loaves and score them with a sharp serrated knife or razor blade, making 2 or 3 diagonal cuts about $1/2$ inch deep.

Transfer the dough to the oven, pour 1 cup of hot water into the steam pan, and lower the oven temperature to 425°F (218°C).

Bake for 15 minutes, then rotate the pans and bake for another 15 to 25 minutes, until the loaves are a deep golden brown and have an internal temperature above 195°F (91°C) in the center.

Remove from the pans and cool on a wire rack for about 1 hour before slicing or serving.

VARIATION

If you would like to avoid the air pockets caused by the melting cheese, you can knead cubed cheese into the dough after the overnight rise, just before shaping, rather than rolling it up in the dough. This will create little cheese bursts throughout the loaf instead of a spiral.

English Muffins

Although store-bought English muffins may look easy to make, they're tricky to do at home, especially if you want to get the spongelike nooks and crannies that trap butter and jam and are the key to their popularity. This version is a cross between a crumpet and a roll. On the inside, it's soft and custardy with lots of pockets, but the outside is chewy and nicely cara-melized. I took inspiration from a recipe I saw on the wonderful e-group *The Bread-Baker's List* (you can sign up at www.bread-bakers.com). That recipe was sent in by Werner Gansz, who clearly spent a lot of time thinking it through. Although this formula is different from his, I thank him for getting me excited about English muffins all over again, and for his inventive method, from which I've borrowed many ideas. Thanks also to recipe tester Lucille Johnston, who made it her personal mission to perfect this recipe.

You'll need crumpet rings or something similar to make these, as the dough is thin and batterlike (it later sets up into a soft, sticky dough), so it must be confined by a form. The rings are readily available at cookware stores, but you can also use the rims of quart-size canning jars. They're shorter than crumpet rings but still work quite well. You'll need to plan ahead in order to follow the process correctly. If you have a flat griddle pan or electric griddle, this is the ideal time to use it, as making these muffins is similar to making pancakes. You can also use a large cast-iron or steel skillet. Other items you'll also need on hand are a metal spatula, and a $1/3$-cup measure for portioning and pouring the dough. Finally, you will need cornmeal to give the tops and bottoms of the English muffins an authentic look.

2 teaspoons (0.5 oz / 14 g) honey

1 tablespoon (0.5 oz / 14 g) vegetable oil or olive oil

$1^{1}/_{2}$ cups (12 oz / 340 g) lukewarm whole or nonfat milk
(about 95°F or 35°C)

$2^{2}/_{3}$ cups (12 oz / 340 g) unbleached bread flour

$3/_{4}$ teaspoon (0.19 oz / 5.5 g) salt, or $1^{1}/_{4}$ teaspoon coarse kosher salt

2 teaspoons (0.22 oz / 6 g) instant yeast

$1/_{4}$ teaspoon (0.06 oz / 2 g) baking soda

3 tablespoons (1.5 oz / 43 g) warm water

Cornmeal, for dusting

DO AHEAD

Add the honey and oil to the milk and stir to dissolve the honey. In a mixing bowl, whisk the flour, salt, and yeast together, then pour in the milk mixture. Whisk for 1 minute, until all of the ingredients are evenly distributed and the flour is hydrated. You should see gluten strands forming as the wet sponge develops. Scrape down the bowl with a spatula, then mix the batter for a few more seconds. Scrape down the bowl again, then cover tightly with plastic wrap and immediately refrigerate overnight or for up to 4 days. The batter will bubble and rise as it cools down.

ON BAKING DAY

Remove the dough from the refrigerator about 2 hours before you plan to bake the English muffins. The dough will be much stiffer but still sticky and it will bubble as it comes to room temperature.

When you're nearly ready to bake, dissolve the baking soda in the warm water and gently fold it into the dough, just like folding egg whites into cake batter, until it is fully absorbed. Let the dough rest for 5 to 10 minutes, until it starts bubbling again. Heat a flat griddle pan or cast-iron skillet over medium heat, or to 300°F (149°C) if using an electric griddle.

Mist the griddle and the inside of the crumpet rings with spray oil, then dust the inside of the rings with cornmeal. Cover the surface of the pan with as many rings as it will hold, then dust the pan inside the rings with more cornmeal. Lower the heat to medium-low, actually closer to low than to medium; you'll have to use trial-and-error on this at first until you find the setting that works with your stove or griddle.

To bake, mist a $^1/_3$-cup measuring cup with spray oil, fill it with dough, and pour the dough into a ring, filling the ring about two-thirds full; depending on the size of the ring, you may not need all of the batter in the scoop to fill each ring, but for standard crumpet rings $^1/_3$ cup of batter is about right. Fill all of the rings, then sprinkle cornmeal over each muffin.

The dough will not spread immediately to fill the ring but will begin to slowly rise and soon will fill and reach the top of the ring; it may or may not bubble. Cook the muffins for at least 12 minutes, or until the bottoms are golden brown and crisp and the tops lose their wet look. Then, flip the muffins over, rings and all, and cook for 12 minutes more. If it takes less than 12 minutes per side, your griddle setting is probably too high and you'll end up with undercooked muffins.

When both sides are golden brown and the dough is springy to the touch, remove the muffins from the pan. Cool them in their rings for about 2 minutes, then pop them out.

Turn the muffins on their edge to cool; this will help prevent sinking and shrinking. Cool for at least 30 minutes before serving. After they cool, you can split them with a fork to accentuate the interior nooks.

VARIATIONS

You can make a partial whole wheat version by using half bread flour and half whole wheat flour. If you do so, increase the amount of milk by $^1/_4$ cup (2 oz / 56.5 g).

You can also substitute $3^1/_2$ teaspoons (0.75 oz / 21 g) of barley malt syrup for the honey if you like.

Soft Pretzels

MAKES 12 TO 17 PRETZELS

There are a number of ways to make pretzels, but I like this version, especially when the pretzels are served with mustard. The baking method is similar to making bagels, but not quite the same. Traditionally, pretzels are dipped in pans of food-grade lye and water to create the distinctive shiny, dark brown crust, but this kind of lye is difficult to obtain and dangerous to have lying around the house, so I suggest substituting a baking soda solution. However, if you can obtain lye and are comfortable using it, follow the instructions on the package. (To use lye crystals, combine 0.75 ounce or 21 grams of crystals with 2 cups of water and be sure to wear protective gloves and eyewear—you can see why I prefer baking soda!)

$4^1/_2$ cups (20 oz / 567 g) unbleached bread flour

$1^3/_4$ teaspoons (0.4 oz / 11 g) salt, or $2^1/_2$ teaspoons coarse kosher salt

$1^1/_2$ tablespoons (0.75 oz / 21 g) brown sugar

1 teaspoon (0.11 oz / 3 g) instant yeast

$1^1/_2$ cups (12 oz / 340 g) lukewarm water (about 95°F or 35°C)

2 tablespoons (1 oz / 28.5 g) vegetable oil or melted unsalted butter

8 teaspoons (2 oz / 57 g) baking soda, for dipping

2 cups (16 oz / 454 g) warm water (about 100°F or 38°C), for dipping

1 egg white, for dipping (optional)

Pretzel salt or coarse sea salt, for garnish

DO AHEAD

Combine the flour, salt, and sugar in a mixing bowl. Whisk the yeast into the lukewarm water until dissolved, then let it sit for 1 minute to hydrate.

Pour the yeast mixture and the oil into the dry ingredients. If using a mixer, use the paddle and mix on the lowest speed for 30 to 60 seconds. If mixing by hand, use a large spoon and stir for about 1 minute. A coarse ball of dough should form.

Switch to the dough hook and mix on the lowest speed, or continue mixing by hand, for 2 minutes. The dough will become slightly smoother. Let the dough rest for 5 minutes.

Continue to mix with the dough hook on medium-low speed, or mix by hand, for 3 minutes, adjusting the water or flour as needed to form a smooth, firm, but slightly tacky ball of dough. If the dough is very tacky or sticky, add more flour.

Transfer the dough to a lightly floured work surface and knead for 1 minute to make any final adjustments. Form the dough into a ball and place it in a clean, lightly oiled bowl. Cover the bowl tightly with plastic wrap and immediately refrigerate overnight or for up to 4 days. (If you plan to bake the dough in batches over different days, you can portion the dough and place it into two or more oiled bowls at this stage.)

ON BAKING DAY

To make the dipping solution, stir the baking soda into the warm water. Whisk in the optional egg white (this will add a little shine, but it's optional).

Preheat the oven to 400°F (204°C). Pour the baking soda solution into a shallow bowl or small pan.

Remove the dough from the refrigerator and immediately divide it into 2-ounce (56.5 g) pieces, or 3-ounce (85 g) pieces if you prefer larger pretzels. Roll each piece into a rope about 17 inches long, tapered at the last 3 inches of each end (if the rope shrinks back after rolling, proceed to the next piece and return a few minutes later, after the gluten has relaxed, and roll the rope again to the full length). Line a sheet pan with parchment paper or a silicone mat. If parchment, mist it with spray oil to prevent sticking. Form each piece of dough into a pretzel shape (see opposite), then place it on the sheet pan.

As soon as the pan is filled, carefully dip each pretzel into the baking soda solution to thoroughly coat it, then put it back on the pan. Sprinkle on salt to taste, but be aware that a little goes a long way. (See the variations below for other garnish suggestions.) Dip and pan all of the pretzels.

Bake for about 8 minutes, then rotate the pan and bake for another 8 to 10 minutes, until the pretzels are a rich brown.

Transfer the pretzels to a wire rack and cool for at least 10 minutes before serving.

VARIATIONS

You can substitute whole grain flour for some of the bread flour. If you do so, add 1 tablespoon (0.5 oz / 14 g) of water to the final dough for every 7 tablespoons (2 oz / 56.5 g) of whole grain flour you use.

You can top these pretzels with many garnishes other than salt. Sesame seeds are very popular, or try savory or spicy seasoning salts or a sweet streusel topping. Another option is to scatter a good melting cheese on the surface for the last 3 minutes of baking. Or, for a decadent delight, drizzle them with chocolate glaze after they come out of the oven and have cooled a bit. (You can use the filling for chocolate croissants, page 189, or use the cinnamon sugar crumb on page 197.)

Shaping Pretzels

Roll each piece of dough into a 17-inch-long rope.

Holding one end of the rope with each hand, cross the strands to make a loop (similar to crossing your hands across your chest). Lay the looped dough on the work surface so the bottom of the loop is closest to you, then cross the strands once more to create an additional twist. Rest the extra strands of the rope on the loop so a small nub of dough overhangs slightly. It should now look like a fairly tight pretzel.

Carefully dip each pretzel into the baking soda solution then place on the pan.

Crispy Rye and Seed Crackers

MAKES 4 PANS OF CRACKERS

Okay, I'll admit it: Although I'm known primarily as a bread guy, I've been eating far more crackers than bread lately—probably always have, actually, and it's a safe bet that I always will. Sure, artisan bread is the sexy sister, but a good cracker is the hardworking Cinderella of baked goods, and I think it's time to bestow the glass slipper. In fact, I have a feeling that there are many other undeclared cracker freaks out there just waiting for crackers to be validated as a significant player in the exploding American culinary renaissance.

A quick look at supermarket shelves shows that the real growth for both crackers and bread is occurring in the whole grain category. Even iconic brands such as Ritz are coming forth with whole grain products. I've spent nearly twenty years trying to convince folks to bake bread at home, even tilting at windmills by trying to encourage them to make 100 percent whole grain breads at home, but I've encountered far less resistance in urging that same audience to try making their own whole grain crackers. Why the receptivity? It's probably because crackers are far easier and faster to make than bread (and the dough doesn't even need to be held overnight in the refrigerator).

But I also think there are deeper reasons. Crackers are so versatile, and so easily substituted for chips and other guilt-laden snacks. Whole grain crackers are the perfect, guilt-free snack. Not only do they have a satisfying, toasty flavor, they're also loaded with dietary fiber, which helps lessen cravings for sweets and reduce mindless eating between meals. When properly made, crackers have a long finish. Eat some now and you'll still be enjoying the lingering, earthy flavors in 30 minutes.

Crackers can be naturally leavened with yeast, like Armenian lavash; be chemically leavened with baking powder or baking soda, like many commercial crackers; or be completely unleavened, like matzo or Triscuits. They're usually crisp and flaky but don't have to be. They can be buttery (with real or fake butter), or lean and mean, like saltines and other variations of water crackers. Whole grain crackers, regardless of the leavening method, have one major factor going for them: fiber, lots and lots of fiber.

This cracker recipe is easy to make at home, even if you've never baked a loaf of bread in your life. It's a variation of one of the most popular recipes from my previous book, *Peter Reinhart's Whole Grain Breads*, and is especially fun to make with kids. I've adjusted the recipe so that these crackers, which are unlike any crackers you can buy, are even more crisp than the original. I'm ready to start a home-baked cracker revolution to match the bread revolution of the last fifteen years and hope I can enlist you in the cause.

1/4 cup (1.5 oz / 42.5 g) sunflower seeds

1/4 cup (1.5 oz / 42.5 g) pumpkin seeds

3 tablespoons (1 oz / 28.5 g) flaxseeds

6 tablespoons (2 oz / 56.5 g) sesame seeds

1 3/4 cups (8 oz / 227 g) rye flour

1/4 teaspoon salt, or 1/3 teaspoon coarse kosher salt

2 tablespoons (1 oz / 28.5 g) vegetable oil

1 tablespoon (0.75 oz / 21 g) honey or agave nectar

3/4 cup (6 oz / 170 g) water, at room temperature

Egg white wash or sweet wash (see sidebar, opposite)

Garnishes (see variations, opposite)

DO AHEAD

Grind the sunflower and pumpkin seeds into a fine powder or flour in a blender or spice grinder. Blend in pulses and be careful not to blend too long, or they'll turn into seed butter. Separately, grind the flaxseeds into a fine powder.

Combine the seed powders and the whole sesame seeds, rye flour, salt, vegetable oil, honey, and water in a mixing bowl. If using a mixer, use the paddle attachment and mix on slow speed for 1 to 2 minutes. If mixing by hand, use a large, sturdy spoon and stir for 1 or 2 minutes. The dough should quickly form a firm ball and shouldn't be sticky. Stir in flour or water as needed to adjust the texture.

Transfer the dough to a lightly floured work surface and knead for about 30 seconds to be sure all of the ingredients are evenly distributed and that the dough holds together. It should be slightly tacky but not sticky.

Preheat the oven to 300°F (149°C), or 275°F (135°C) for a convection oven, and prepare 1 baking sheet for each quarter of the dough that you plan to bake, lining them with parchment paper or a silicone mat. You don't need to oil the paper or liner.

Divide the dough into four equal pieces. (For any that you won't be baking right away, wrap them well, and refrigerate for up to 1 week or freeze for up to 3 months; the flavor actually improves after a day or two in the refrigerator.) Use a rolling pin to roll out one portion of the dough on a floured work surface, frequently lifting the dough with a metal pastry scraper or bowl scraper to be sure it isn't sticking and dusting with more flour underneath if need be. You can also flip the dough over and continue rolling with the bottom side up. The goal is to roll it to about $^1/_{16}$ inch in thickness. If the dough resists, gently set it aside and begin rolling out another piece, or let it rest for about 2 minutes. When you return to it, it will roll more easily.

FINISHING THE DOUGH AND BAKING

Brush the surface of the dough with an even coating of whichever wash you prefer, then sprinkle the surface with whatever garnishes you like (see the variations below).

Use a pizza cutter to cut the rolled dough into rectangles, diamonds, or other shapes. You can also use a small biscuit cutter dipped in flour to make round crackers, but this takes longer, and then you have leftover dough. The crackers need not all be the same size. Transfer the crackers to the prepared pan. They can be nearly touching, as they won't spread or rise.

If making more than one pan of crackers, you can bake them all at once. Place the pans on different shelves and bake for 10 minutes, then rotate the pans and bake for another 10 minutes. Rotate the pans once more and continue baking until they're done—typically 25 to 30 minutes altogether, but it depends on how thin you roll them and on your oven. The crackers are done when they have a rich golden brown color and are fairly dry and crisp. Leave them on the pans to cool so they'll crisp up even more. To get a little more browning on the crackers, increase the heat to 325°F (163°C) after they've dried sufficiently to be crisp (20 to 25 minutes). If they don't snap cleanly after they cool, return the pan to a hot oven for a few more minutes until they dry sufficiently to snap when broken.

Cool for at least 15 minutes before serving. Once thoroughly cooled, the crackers can be stored in an airtight container at room temperature for about 8 days, or in a ziplock bag in the freezer indefinitely.

VARIATIONS

Sesame seeds and poppy seeds are the best garnishing seeds because they're light, and because their flavor isn't so strong that they'll overpower the taste of the cracker, as something like cumin or anise seeds would. Flaxseeds are a little too hard to chew, especially when baked on top of crackers, but some people do like them as a garnish. Other savory garnishes

Garnishing Washes

To make the garnishes stick to the dough, you need either an egg white wash for savory crackers or a sweet wash for seeds or a sweet garnish. To make the egg wash, whisk 1 egg white with 2 tablespoons of water. To make the sweet wash, whisk 1 tablespoon of honey or agave nectar with 3 tablespoons of water.

include garlic salt, lemon pepper, and other common spice blends and rubs. You can make wonderful toppings by combining herbs and oil, such as herbes de Provence covered with just enough oil to make a paste. In this case, don't use a glaze; simply brush the oil on the cracker dough just prior to baking. Flavored herb and garlic oils can also be brushed onto the crackers as soon as they come out of the oven, to shine them up and add flavor. If you try this, return the crackers to the oven for 5 minutes more to set the glaze.

This recipe uses rye flour for a unique flavor, but you can substitute either regular whole wheat flour or the newly popular white whole wheat flour, which is a lighter color and has a slightly sweeter, less bitter flavor than traditional red wheat. You can also use all-purpose flour if you prefer a lighter cracker, and reduce the water by 1 tablespoon for every 2 ounces of white flour that you substitute.

Flaky, Buttery Crackers

MAKES 4 PANS OF CRACKERS

This recipe makes a home-baked cracker similar to the famous, wonderfully buttery tasting Ritz brand crackers. Recipe tester Pamela Schmidt, who worked long and hard on this one, determined that a little garlic powder in the dough made these taste even more like Ritz crackers. I don't know if Ritz actually puts garlic powder in their version, but it does add a nice flavor, so I'm going with Pamela on this one.

1¼ cups (5.5 oz / 156 g) all-purpose flour
1 cup (4.5 oz / 128 g) cake flour
1 teaspoon (0.25 oz / 7 g) salt, or 1½ teaspoons coarse kosher salt
1 tablespoon (0.5 oz / 14 g) sugar
¾ teaspoon (0.18 oz / 5.25 g) baking powder
½ teaspoon (0.13 oz / 3.5 g) garlic powder
10 tablespoons (5 oz / 142 g) melted unsalted butter or vegetable oil, plus 4 tablespoons (2 oz / 57 g) melted unsalted butter for garnishing (optional)
1 egg (1.75 oz / 50 g)
6 tablespoons (3 oz / 85 g) cold milk (any kind)
Egg wash (see page 135)

Combine all of the ingredients, except the optional butter for garnishing and the egg wash, in a mixing bowl. If using a mixer, mix with the paddle attachment on low speed for 1 minute. If mixing by hand, use a large, sturdy spoon and mix for 1 minute. The dough should form a firm ball and shouldn't be sticky. Stir in flour or water as needed to adjust the texture.

Transfer the dough to a lightly floured work surface and knead for about 30 seconds to be sure all of the ingredients are evenly distributed and that the dough holds together. It should be slightly tacky but not sticky.

Preheat the oven to 400°F (204°C), or 350°F (175°C) for a convection oven, and line 2 baking sheets with parchment paper or a silicone mat. You don't need to oil the paper or liner.

Use a rolling pin to roll out the dough on the floured work surface, frequently lifting the dough with a metal pastry scraper or bowl scraper to be sure it isn't sticking and dusting with more flour underneath if need be. You can also flip the dough over and continue rolling with the bottom side up. The goal is to roll it to about $1/8$ inch in thickness. Use a fork or dough docker (a roller device with studs) and poke holes all over the surface of the dough. Brush the surface of the dough with an even coating of the egg wash and sprinkle with fine salt.

FINISHING THE DOUGH AND BAKING

Use a small biscuit cutter (a crimped cutter is preferred but not required) dipped in flour to make round crackers. Place the crackers about $1/2$ inch apart on one of the prepared pans. Gather any scrap dough and repeat the rolling out, egg wash, and garnishing process until all the dough is formed into crackers. (You can also cut the dough with a pizza cutter into rectangles or diamonds, if you prefer.)

If making more than one pan of crackers, you can bake them all at once. Place the pans on different shelves and bake for 8 minutes, then rotate the pans and bake for another 8 to 12 minutes, or until the crackers are firm and lightly golden. Remove the pans from the oven and brush the hot crackers with the melted butter, if garnishing. Immediately, turn off the oven, then return the pans to the hot oven for 3 to 5 minutes. Remove the pans from the oven and let the crackers cool on the pan. The crackers are done when they have a rich golden brown color and are fairly dry and crisp. If they don't snap cleanly after they cool, return the pan to a hot oven for a few more minutes until they dry sufficiently to snap when broken.

CHAPTER 5

Rich Breads

Rich breads are the privileged cousins of enriched breads, as they are much higher in fat and, sometimes, sugar. Butter is the fat of choice, here, though other fats will work, including vegetable oil. These breads are usually made for special occasions, as they require careful attention at almost every stage: mixing, shaping, and baking. Rich breads are generally defined as having at least 10 percent fat and/or sweetener (in ratio to the flour), but are often much richer than that. The abundance of enrichments helps to create a tender, buttery texture and mouthfeel, as well as to impart a deep and abiding sense of satisfaction.

Fruit-filled thumbprint rolls (page 152)

Cinnamon Buns

The simple, sweet enriched dough for these cinnamon buns is very versatile. It can also be used to make to make everything from sticky buns (page 145) and coffee crumb cake (page 150) to fruit-filled thumbprint pastries (page 152). Even though this dough doesn't contain eggs, it can still make all of these products, and more, but with less work and fewer calories than some of the richer recipes that follow. I wouldn't exactly call this health food, but anything made with this dough is definitely comfort food to the max!

I've suggested chopped walnuts or pecans, but feel free to experiment with other nuts. I've given you the option of either a cream cheese frosting or a fondant glaze, both of which are delicious and commonly used in pastry shops. The corn syrup in the fondant glaze is optional, but using it will make the glaze smoother. Using milk, rather than water, in the fondant will also make it creamier and softer.

ALL-PURPOSE SWEET DOUGH

6¼ cups (28 oz / 794 g) unbleached all-purpose flour

2 teaspoons (0.5 oz / 14 g) salt, or 1 tablespoon coarse kosher salt

6 tablespoons (3 oz / 85 g) sugar

5 teaspoons (0.55 oz / 15.5 g) instant yeast

2 cups plus 2 tablespoons (17 oz / 482 g) lukewarm whole or low-fat milk (about 95°F or 35°C)

½ cup (4 oz / 113 g) vegetable oil or melted unsalted butter

Zest of ½ lemon, or 1 tablespoon lemon extract, or ½ teaspoon lemon oil (optional)

TOPPING

3 tablespoons (1.5 oz / 43 g) ground cinnamon

¾ cup (6 oz / 170 g) sugar

Melted butter or vegetable oil, for brushing

1 cup (6 oz / 170 g) raisins, or to taste (optional)

1 cup (5 oz / 142 g) chopped walnuts or pecans, or to taste (optional)

To make the dough, combine the flour, salt, and sugar in a mixing bowl. Whisk the yeast into the milk until dissolved, then pour the mixture into the dry ingredients, along with the oil and lemon zest. If using a mixer, use the paddle attachment and mix on the lowest speed for 30 seconds to 1 minute. If mixing by hand, use a large spoon and stir for about 1 minute. The dough should form a soft, coarse ball.

Switch to the dough hook and mix on medium-low speed, or continue mixing by hand, for 4 minutes, adding flour or milk as needed to create a smooth, soft, slightly sticky ball of dough.

Increase the speed to medium and mix for 2 minutes more or continue stirring for about 2 minutes more, until the dough is very soft, supple, and tacky but not sticky.

Transfer the dough to a lightly floured work surface and knead for 1 minute, then form it into a ball.

Place the dough in a clean, lightly oiled bowl large enough to hold the dough when it doubles in size. Cover the bowl tightly with plastic wrap, and refrigerate overnight or for up to 4 days.

ON BAKING DAY

Remove the dough from the refrigerator about 3 hours before you plan to bake. Divide the dough in half and form each piece into a ball. Cover each ball with a bowl or plastic wrap and let rest for 20 minutes.

On a floured work surface, roll each ball of dough into a 12 by 15-inch rectangle, rolling from the center to the corners and then rolling out to the sides. If the dough starts to resist or shrink back, let it rest for 1 minute, then continue rolling. The dough should be between $1/4$ and $1/2$ inch thick.

Make cinnamon sugar by whisking the cinnamon into the sugar. Brush the surface of the dough with melted butter, then sprinkle the cinnamon sugar over the surface, leaving a $1/4$-inch border. Sprinkle the raisins, chopped nuts, or both over the surface if you like, to taste. Roll up the dough like a rug, rolling from the bottom to the top, to form a tight log.

Cut the log into 1-inch-thick slices and place them on a sheet pan or two round cake pans lined with parchment paper or a silicone mat, placing the rolls about $1^{1}/_{2}$ inches apart; they should touch each other once they rise. Mist the tops with spray oil and cover loosely with plastic wrap, then let rise at room temperature for about 2 hours, until the dough swells noticeably and the buns begin to expand into each other.

About 15 minutes before baking, preheat the oven to 350°F (177°C).

Bake for 10 minutes, then rotate the pan and bake for another 5 to 15 minutes, until the buns are a rich golden brown. Meanwhile, make whichever topping you prefer.

Once the buns are glazed, enjoy!

Topping Options

CREAM CHEESE FROSTING

4 ounces (113 g) cream cheese

$1/4$ cup (2 oz / 56.5 g) melted unsalted butter

1 cup (3 oz / 85 g) confectioners' sugar, sifted

1 teaspoon (0.25 oz / 7 g) vanilla extract

$1/4$ teaspoon (0.25 oz / 7 g) lemon or orange extract,
or 1 teaspoon (0.25 oz / 7 g) lemon juice or orange liqueur

Pinch of salt

Combine the cream cheese, butter, and sugar in a mixing bowl. If using a mixer, use the paddle attachment and mix on the lowest speed for 2 minutes. If mixing by hand, stir vigorously for 2 to 4 minutes. The ingredients should be evenly incorporated and smooth. Add the vanilla, lemon extract, and salt and mix on medium speed, or continue mixing by hand, for about 1 minute, until the ingredients form a smooth paste. Increase the speed to medium-high or stir more vigorously for about 20 seconds to fluff up the glaze. Once the buns have cooled for 5 minutes, use an offset spatula or a table knife to spread on however much glaze you'd like. Stored in an airtight container in the refrigerator; any unused glaze will keep for up to 2 weeks.

WHITE FONDANT GLAZE

4 cups (12 oz / 340 g) confectioners' sugar, sifted
2 tablespoons (1.5 oz / 43 g) light corn syrup (optional)
1 teaspoon (0.25 oz / 7 g) vanilla, lemon, or orange extract, or 1 tablespoon (0.75 oz / 21 g) orange juice concentrate (optional)
$^1/_2$ to $^3/_4$ cup (4 to 6 ounces / 113 to 170 g) milk or water

Stir the sugar, corn syrup, and vanilla together. Gradually whisk in the milk, adding just enough to make a thick but creamy glaze about the same thickness as pancake batter, adjusting with more liquid or sugar as needed. The thickness of the glaze is up to you; the stiffer it is, the better it will hold its design; the thinner it is, the more easily it will spread. Ideally, you should be able to drizzle a slow steady stream off the end of a spoon or other utensil to create designs that will firm up when the buns cool. Glaze the buns after they've cooled for about 5 minutes.

Sticky Buns

MAKES 24 STICKY BUNS

For sticky buns, be sure to use pans with at least 2-inch-high walls, as the slurry will bubble and foam while baking and could overflow a pan with a shallow rim. Place the pans on a sheet pan to catch any glaze that does bubble over. I've given you three options for the sweet slurry in the bottom of the pan. Each is delicious, so you'll just have to give them all a try and see which you prefer. Thanks to recipe tester Jim Lee for the delicious creamy caramel slurry recipe, a classic cream and sugar version, which is very easy to make. His caramel is different in texture and color from Susan's (my wife's no-longer-secret recipe!), which is made from a sugar and butter combination, but both result in serious childhood flashbacks. If you use the honey almond slurry, yet another wonderful glaze, it would be a good idea to use slivered or coarsely chopped almonds if you sprinkle nuts over the dough before rolling it up. Whichever version you use, the uncooked slurry should cover the bottom of the pan to a thickness of about 1/4 inch.

1 recipe all-purpose sweet dough (page 140)
3 tablespoons (1.5 oz / 42 g) ground cinnamon
3/4 cup (6 oz / 170 g) sugar
Melted butter or vegetable oil, for brushing
1 cup (6 oz / 170 g) raisins, or to taste (optional)
1 cup (5 oz / 142 g) chopped walnuts or pecans, or to taste (optional)

Prepare the all-purpose sweet dough as directed on page 140.

ON BAKING DAY

Remove the sweet dough from the refrigerator about 3 hours before you plan to bake. Divide it in half and form each piece into a ball. Cover each ball with a bowl or plastic wrap and let rest for 20 minutes.

On a floured work surface, roll each ball of dough into a 12 by 15-inch rectangle, rolling from the center to the corners and then rolling out to the sides. If the dough starts to resist or shrink back, let it rest for 1 minute, then continue rolling. The dough should be between 1/4 and 1/2 inch thick.

Make cinnamon sugar by whisking the cinnamon into the sugar. Brush the surface of the dough with melted butter, then sprinkle the cinnamon sugar over the surface, leaving a 1/4-inch border. Sprinkle the raisins, chopped nuts, or both over the surface if you like. Roll up the dough like a rug, rolling from the bottom to the top to form a tight log. Make one of the slurries.

Fill the bottom of two 8- or 9-inch round pans or one 12-inch square pan with 1/4 inch of one of the slurries. Store any excess slurry in the refrigerator, where it will keep for at least 2 weeks. Sprinkle chopped nuts over the slurry if you like; although this is optional, it's highly advised for flavor.

Cut the log into 1-inch slices and place them on the slurry with the nicest side down, leaving about 1 inch of space between the buns. Mist with spray oil and cover loosely with plastic wrap, then let rise at room temperature for about 2 hours, until the dough swells noticeably and the buns begin to expand into each other.

About 15 minutes before baking, put the oven rack in a low position (so the slurry gets plenty of bottom heat) and preheat the oven to 350°F (177°C).

Bake for 20 to 25 minutes, rotating the pans as needed for an even bake. The slurry will melt, bubble, and caramelize, and the visible dough will be a dark golden brown. Lift one of the buns with a metal spatula or a pair of tongs to check the underside of the dough, which should be a light caramel brown, not white. The sugar slurry should turn a rich amber or golden brown, and all of the sugar should have melted to become caramel. (If it is still grainy and not amber, continue baking; you can put a tent of aluminum foil over the buns to protect them from getting too dark while the slurry finishes caramelizing.)

Remove the pans from the oven and let the buns cool for 2 to 3 minutes in the pans so the caramel begins to firm up. Place a platter or pan over the top of the baking pan. It should be large enough to cover the baking pan and hold all of the buns. Wearing oven mitts or using hot pads, flip the entire assemblage over to release the buns and caramel onto the platter. Be careful, the glaze will still be very hot at this point. Use a rubber spatula to scrape any remaining glaze from the pan and drizzle it over the tops of the buns.

Cool for at least 15 minutes before serving.

continued

A nice addition is to sprinkle about $^1/_2$ cup (3 oz / 85 g) of raisins, dried cranberries, or other dried fruit over the slurry before placing the rolls in the pan. If using larger dried fruits, such as dried apricots, chop them into small bits first.

You can also bake the buns in greased muffin tins. Put $^1/_4$ inch of slurry in each cup, sprinkle in nuts or dried fruit as you wish, then press in a slice of the rolled dough. You'll probably need to slice the log thinner than 1 inch so that the spirals fill the muffin cups half full. Proof and bake as directed above.

Slurry Options

CREAMY CARAMEL SLURRY

$^1/_2$ cup (4 oz / 113 g) granulated sugar
$^1/_2$ cup (4 oz / 113 g) light brown sugar
$^1/_2$ cup (4 oz / 113 g) heavy or whipping cream
1 tablespoon (0.5 oz / 14 g) unsalted butter, melted or at room temperature
1 tablespoon (0.75 oz / 21 g) light corn syrup

Combine all of the ingredients in a mixing bowl. If using a mixer, use the paddle attachment and mix on medium speed for 1 to 2 minutes . If mixing by hand, stir vigorously with a large spoon for about 2 minutes. The mixture should be smooth and homogeneous.

HONEY ALMOND SLURRY

1 cup (12 oz / 340 g) honey
1 cup (8 oz / 227 g) unsalted butter, melted or at room temperature
$^1/_4$ teaspoon salt, or $^3/_8$ teaspoon coarse kosher salt
1 teaspoon (0.25 oz / 7 g) almond extract

Combine all of the ingredients in a mixing bowl. If using a mixer, use the paddle attachment and mix on medium-high speed for about 2 minutes. If mixing by hand, stir vigorously with a large spoon for about 2 minutes. The mixture should be smooth and homogeneous.

$1/2$ cup (4 oz / 113 g) granulated sugar

$1/2$ cup (4 oz / 113 g) light brown sugar

$1/2$ cup (4 oz / 113 g) unsalted butter, melted or at room temperature

2 tablespoons (1.5 oz / 43 g) light corn syrup

$1/4$ teaspoon salt, or $3/8$ teaspoon coarse kosher salt

$1/2$ teaspoon (0.13 oz / 3.5 g) lemon or orange extract (optional)

Combine the sugars and butter in a mixing bowl. If using a mixer, use the paddle attachment and mix on medium speed for 2 minutes. If mixing by hand, stir vigorously with a large spoon for 2 minutes. The ingredients should be smooth and evenly blended. Add the corn syrup, salt, and lemon extract and mix with the paddle attachment on medium speed, or continue mixing vigorously by hand, for about 2 minutes. Increase to medium-high speed or stir even more vigorously for 1 or 2 minutes, until the slurry is fluffy.

Coffee Crumb Cake

1 recipe all-purpose sweet dough (page 140)

CRUMB TOPPING

1 cup (4.5 oz / 128 g) all-purpose flour

1 cup (8 oz / 113 g) light brown sugar

$1/8$ teaspoon salt

$1/4$ teaspoon ground cinnamon

$1/8$ teaspoon of one other spice such as nutmeg, allspice, cloves, cardamom, or ground ginger (optional)

$1/2$ cup (4 oz / 113 g) melted unsalted butter

DO AHEAD

Prepare the all-purpose sweet dough as directed on page 140.

ON BAKING DAY

Remove the dough from the refrigerator about 2 hours before you plan to bake. Prepare a 12 by 16-inch pan if baking all of the dough (about 36 ounces, or 1.02 kg), or a 9-inch round pan if baking a smaller amount (about 12 ounces, or 340 g), by lining with parchment paper or a silicone mat, then generously greasing with vegetable oil or melted butter. Dip your fingertips in a small dish of vegetable oil or melted butter, then use your fingertips to dimple the dough and spread it to cover the sheet pan as fully and evenly as possible, much as you would for pressing out focaccia. If the dough resists or starts to shrink back, give it 20 minutes to rest, then dimple and spread it again. Each time you dimple the dough, it should cover the pan more completely, but it may take 3 pressings to spread it fully. Cover the pan loosely with plastic wrap and let the dough rise at room temperature for about 2 hours, until doubled in size. It should rise to a height of 1 inch to $1^1/2$ inches.

To make the crumb topping, whisk the flour, sugar, salt, cinnamon, and other spice together, then pour in the melted butter. Stir with a large spoon, then switch to mixing with your fingers to make streusel-like crumbles. Cover the dough with the crumb topping.

About 15 minutes before baking, preheat the oven to 350°F (177°C).

Bake for 15 minutes, then rotate the pan and bake for another 10 to 20 minutes, until the crumb topping is golden brown and the dough underneath is springy to the touch. The total baking time will vary depending on the size of the pan, so watch the coffee cake closely toward the end of the baking time.

Cool in the pan for 30 to 45 minutes before cutting into squares or wedges and serving.

VARIATIONS

Consider adding chopped nuts, fresh or frozen fruit, or both to the crumb topping. Choose whatever nuts or fruit you like; I recommend blueberries, peaches, mango, or pineapple. (Cut larger fruits into small chunks.)

Another option is to top the coffee cake with a drizzle of white fondant glaze (see page 144) after it cools. Or, for a simple but popular garnish, dust the top with confectioners' sugar.

Fruit-Filled Thumbprint Rolls

MAKES UP TO 36 ROLLS

Feel free to be creative with the fillings for these delicious pastries, which are similar to kolaches. I have suggested a couple of fillings below, which are also excellent for Danish, but you can also use store-bought pie fillings.

1 recipe all-purpose sweet dough (page 140)

1 recipe fruit filling (page 196) or lemon curd (page 196),
or 1 can commercial pie filling

1 recipe white fondant glaze (page 144)

DO AHEAD

Prepare the all-purpose sweet dough as directed on page 140.

ON BAKING DAY

Preheat the oven to 375°F (191°C). Remove the dough from the refrigerator and divide it into $1^1/_2$-ounce pieces. Form each piece into a tight round roll (see page 25), then place the rolls on a parchment-lined sheet pan, about $1^1/_2$ inches apart. Mist the tops of the rolls with spray oil and cover loosely with plastic wrap. Proof at room temperature for about 2 hours, until the rolls have increased to about $1^1/_2$ times their original size.

Dip your thumb in water, then use it to press a deep dimple into each roll. Press almost to the bottom of the dough and rotate your thumb to widen the dimple to about 1 inch across. The roll will spread slightly. Fill the thumbprint with the filling of your choice, and feel free to use a variety of fillings so that you'll have an assortment of rolls.

Bake for 15 to 20 minutes, until a golden brown, rotating the pan as necessary for even browning. As soon as the rolls come out of the oven, brush them with the fondant glaze (which will melt) and let cool for 5 minutes. Then drizzle more glaze over the tops of the rolls while they're still slightly warm, to create decorative streaks.

Serve warm or cold.

Chocolate Cinnamon Babka

MAKES 1 LARGE LOAF

Babka is a rich, yeasted cross between bread and coffee cake with an equally rich Russian and Polish culinary heritage. The name is derived from the Russian *baba*, which means grandmother, an appropriate name for this wonderful comfort food. While it is mostly known as a popular Jewish bread filled with some combination of chocolate, cinnamon, almonds, even poppy seeds and sometimes topped with streusel, it can also be filled with raisins or soaked with rum, as in *baba au rhum.* The dough is rich enough that it can also be used for brioche and *kugelhopf.* In American bakeries, babka is most often formed as a twisted loaf with veins of the sweet filling running throughout, baked either in a loaf pan or freestanding. However, the Israeli version, known as *kranz* cake, uses a dramatic shaping technique that many of my recipe testers found appealing.

This recipe is my favorite version, with both cinnamon and chocolate in the filling. Of course, you can leave out the chocolate and make a cinnamon sugar version, or leave out the cinnamon and make just a chocolate version, but I say, why leave out either? It's easier to grind the chocolate chips or chunks if they're frozen. After you grind them, you can add the cinnamon and butter and continue to process them all together. The streusel topping is also optional, but I highly recommend using it on the freestanding versions.

2 tablespoons (0.66 oz / 19 g) instant yeast

$^3/_4$ cup (6 oz / 170 g) lukewarm milk (any kind; at about 95°F or 35°C)

6 tablespoons (3 oz / 85 g) unsalted butter, melted
or at room temperature

6 tablespoons (3 oz / 85 g) sugar

1 teaspoon (0.25 oz / 7 g) vanilla extract

4 egg yolks (3 oz / 85 g)

3$^1/_3$ cups (15 oz / 425 g) unbleached all-purpose flour

1 teaspoon (0.25 oz / 7 g) salt, or 1$^1/_2$ teaspoons coarse kosher salt

1 egg, for egg wash (if using streusel topping)

1 tablespoon water, for egg wash
(if using streusel topping)

continued

1¹/₂ cups (9 oz / 255 g) frozen semisweet dark chocolate chips or chunks

1 teaspoon (0.25 oz / 7 g) ground cinnamon

¹/₄ cup (2 oz / 56.5 g) cold unsalted butter

STREUSEL TOPPING (OPTIONAL)

¹/₄ cup (2 oz / 56.5 g) cold unsalted butter

¹/₂ cup (2.25 oz / 64 g) all-purpose flour

¹/₂ cup (4 oz / 113 g) brown sugar

Pinch of salt

¹/₄ teaspoon ground cinnamon (optional)

DO AHEAD

Whisk the yeast into the lukewarm milk until dissolved, then set it aside for about 5 minutes before mixing it into the dough.

Cream the butter and sugar together until smooth. If using a mixer, use the paddle attachment and mix on medium speed for 1 to 2 minutes. If mixing by hand, use a large wooden spoon and beat vigorously for about 2 minutes. Add the vanilla to the egg yolks and whisk lightly to break up the yolks, then add the yolks to the sugar mixture in four portions, mixing until each is incorporated before adding the next. Increase the mixer speed to medium-high or continue mixing by hand for another 2 minutes, until the mixture is fluffy, scraping down the sides of the bowl a couple of times during the process.

Stop mixing and add the flour and salt, then pour in the milk mixture. Resume mixing at low speed, or continue to stir by hand, for 2 to 3 minutes, to make a soft, supple, tacky dough. If using a mixer and the mixer begins to struggle, switch to the dough hook; if mixing by hand, use a very sturdy spoon or your hands.

Transfer the dough to a floured work surface and knead by hand for 2 minutes more, adding more flour as needed to make the dough pliable. The dough should be a beautiful golden color and feel soft and supple. Form the dough into a ball.

Place the dough in a clean, lightly oiled bowl, cover the bowl tightly with plastic wrap, and leave at room temperature for about 2¹/₂ hours. It will rise somewhat, but won't double in size. If it rises significantly in less time, you can move to the shaping step or place it in the refrigerator overnight to be rolled out the next day.

Kneading Rich Dough

The dough is soft and supple, and is easy to knead by hand.

Prepare the filling while the dough is rising. Grind the chocolate in a food processor until it's nearly powdered; if you don't have a food processor, chop the chocolate as fine as possible with a knife or metal pastry scraper. Add the cinnamon and pulse or stir a time or two to incorporate. Cut the butter into 8 to 10 pieces, add it to the food processor, and pulse until the butter is evenly dispersed into the chocolate mixture; or cut the butter into the chocolate mixture with a metal pastry scraper to make a streusel-like chocolate crumble.

Once the dough has risen, roll it into a 15 by 15-inch square on a lightly floured surface. It should be between $1/4$ and $1/8$ inch thick. As you roll, frequently lift the dough with a metal pastry scraper or bowl scraper and dust with more flour underneath to prevent sticking. Sprinkle the chocolate mixture over the dough, breaking up any clumps, so the filling covers the surface of the dough evenly, leaving a $1/4$-inch border.

Roll up the dough like a jelly roll and place it seam side down on the work surface. With firm but gentle pressure, rock the log back and forth to extend its length until it is 18 to 24 inches long.

For a loaf shape, grease a 5 by 9-inch loaf pan. Carefully twist the log from both ends without tearing it, just enough to accentuate the chocolate spiral. Coil the log into a circular snail shape, then stand the coil on its end so it's perpendicular to the counter rather than lying flat. Press down on the coil to compress it into a loaf shape. Place it in the greased loaf pan or on a parchment-lined sheet pan with the smoothest, domed side up. For a coffee cake style of babka, grease a tube pan such as a Bundt pan or *kugelhopf* mold with butter, vegetable oil, or spray oil, making sure to grease the tube. Wrap the log around the tube and press the dough into the pan to connect the ends of the log. (Or you can use the Israeli *kranz* cake shaping method, as shown in the photos on page 159.)

Cover the tube or loaf pan loosely with plastic wrap and let the dough rise at room temperature for 2 to 3 hours, until the babka fills the pan or has increased to about 1¹/₂ times its original size. At this point, you can proceed directly to baking or refrigerate the babka overnight. If holding it overnight, remove the dough from the refrigerator about 2 hours before you plan to bake it.

Preheat the oven to 350°F (177°C). Use a toothpick to poke a few holes in the top of the babka to eliminate possible air pockets between the layers of chocolate and dough.

While the oven preheats, make the streusel if you'd like to use it. Combine all of the ingredients in a food processor and pulse to combine, or cut the butter into small bits, then add the other ingredients and stir or mix with your hands. The texture should resemble cornmeal. If using streusel, brush the top of the babka with egg wash (see page 135), then scatter the streusel over the top.

Bake for 20 to 25 minutes, then rotate the pan and bake until the top is a rich dark brown, the sides are a rich golden brown, the loaf sounds hollow when thumped on the bottom, and the internal temperature is about 185°F (85°C) in the center. The babka will begin to brown quickly because of the sugar, but it won't burn. The total baking time is 50 to 60 minutes for a loaf, and just 35 to 45 minutes for a tube pan. The sides may feel soft because of air pockets in the spirals. The babka will soften as it cools.

Cool for at least 90 minutes before serving. The babka is best served at room temperature after the chocolate has had time to set.

VARIATIONS

You can use almond paste in place of the chocolate filling, or simply add sliced almonds to the chocolate filling.

continued

Another nice variation is adding 1¹/₂ cups (9 oz / 255 g) of golden raisins, dried cherries, or dried cranberries and 1 teaspoon of orange zest to the dough during the final minute of mixing. For an added treat, soak the dried fruit in ³/₄ cup (6 oz / 170 g) of rum or brandy overnight before adding it to the dough, as you might for panettone or stollen.

An alternative method for preparing the filling is to barely melt the chocolate, cinnamon, and butter in a double boiler or microwave, then stir the ingredients together and form them into a pliable 16-inch square on a sheet of parchment paper that has been misted with spray oil. Cool this chocolate square in the refrigerator until it is firm. You can transfer this sheet of chocolate directly on top of the babka dough after you roll it out.

Kranz Cake Babka

You can prepare the chocolate filling by spreading the barely-melted mixture on a sheet of parchment paper or silicone baking mat, then refrigerating it until firm.

Cover the rolled out dough with the chocolate (using either the sheet method or the sprinkle method), then roll the dough into a log. Using a metal pastry blade, cut the log down the middle lengthwise. Cross one piece over the other, then continue to criss-cross the pieces in both directions to form a braid (see page 97 for more on 2-braid loaves).

RICH HOLIDAY BREADS

There are so many breads associated with festivals and holidays that entire books, like Betsy Oppenneer's *Celebration Breads,* have been written on the subject. To do justice to these breads and remain true to the story and symbolism of each one truly requires a specific recipe for each bread. However, since I'm exploring these breads in terms of their dough category (rich holiday breads), I've created a general master formula, based on the ratio of ingredients and enrichments, to produce versions of many regional specialties. The acidity of the sourdough starter adds both flavor and textural qualities and also serves as a natural preservative. The mixed method of fermentation differentiates this dough from versions typically used in these breads. The mixing method is rather demanding, requiring gradual additions of the sugar, and then gradual additions of the butter; this dough definitely isn't fast, but it isn't very difficult to make if you take your time.

This formula is quite versatile and can be used to make Italian *pandoro* and panettone, as well as German (Dresden-style) stollen, Greek Christmas or Easter bread, hot cross buns, and even brioche and a variation of babka. The basic dough can be kept in the refrigerator for up to 4 days before shaping and baking, but it's best when panned on the same day it's mixed, after one long rise. Possibilities for the addition of fruit, nuts, and fillings are endless, as are the potential shaping methods. The shapes shown here are a starting point; feel free to play with them and try other shapes, both traditional and innovative.

Clockwise from top: brioche à tête (page 167), mini panettone (page 163), hot cross bun (page 172), stollen (page 168)

Panettone

Panettone is the famous Christmas bread of Milan, though it is now made and consumed year round. *Pandoro*, or "golden bread," originated in Verona and is traditionally baked in star-shaped molds, but otherwise bears strong similarities to its more well-known Milanese counterpart. Although this dough can be mixed by hand, it's very hard to do so because of the long mixing time required, so I recommend using a stand mixer. (You could also use a food processor if you pulse, rather than processing for extended periods.) At first, the dough will be more like a batter, but as you scrape down the mixing bowl, it will eventually form a very supple, delicate dough that feels wonderful to the touch. It can be formed into a ball or other bread shapes, but if you squeeze too hard it will become loose and sticky again.

You may want to purchase paper or metal panettone or *pandoro* molds, which are available at specialty cookware stores. Keep in mind that smaller loaves bake more quickly and are softer and less crusty than larger loaves. Muffin and popover pans, as well as small brioche cups, make nice molds for mini loaves, as do small cans. You'll end up with a better loaf if you let the dough rise slowly at room temperature rather than force the rise (for example, by placing the dough in a pilot-lit oven, which is a tempting way to speed up the rising time for many doughs). It may take up to 12 hours for the dough to rise and fill the form, but it's worth the wait. Warmer proofing risks melting the butter in the dough, so the finished product will have the structure of a *kugelhopf* coffee cake—which isn't bad, but it doesn't have the unique peel-apart qualities of the slower-rising panettone or *pandoro*.

SOURDOUGH STARTER

3 tablespoons (1.5 oz / 42.5 g) mother starter (page 42), cold or at room temperature

1¹/₃ cups (6 oz / 170 g) unbleached bread flour

¹/₄ cup plus 2 tablespoons (3 oz / 85 g) water, at room temperature

DOUGH

All of the sourdough starter (9 oz / 255 g)

1 tablespoon (0.75 oz / 21 g) honey

¹/₄ cup (2 oz / 56.5 g) lukewarm water (about 95°F or 35°C)

1 teaspoon (0.11 oz / 3 g) instant yeast

continued

1 egg (1.75 oz / 50 g), at room temperature

3 egg yolks (2.25 oz / 65 g), at room temperature

1 tablespoon (0.5 oz / 14 g) vanilla extract

1²/₃ cups (7.5 oz / 213 g) unbleached bread flour
or high-gluten flour

³/₄ teaspoon (0.21 oz / 4 g) salt, or 1¹/₄ teaspoon coarse kosher salt

3 tablespoons (1.5 oz / 43 g) sugar

³/₄ cup (6 oz / 170 g) unsalted butter, at room temperature

1¹/₃ cups (8 oz / 227 g) dried or candied fruit
(optional; see variations on page 166 for full details)

DO AHEAD

To make the starter, combine all of the ingredients in a mixing bowl. If using a mixer, use the paddle attachment and mix on the lowest speed for 1 minute, then increase to medium speed for about 30 seconds. If mixing by hand, stir for about 2 minutes, until well blended. The starter should feel doughlike and tacky or slightly sticky; if not, stir in additional flour or water as needed.

Transfer the starter to a lightly floured work surface and knead for about 30 seconds. Place the starter in a clean, lightly oiled bowl, cover the bowl loosely, and leave at room temperature

for 6 to 8 hours, until the starter doubles in size or swells considerably. You can use it immediately or put it in the refrigerator for up to 4 days.

To make the dough, cut the starter into 10 to 12 pieces and put the pieces in a mixing bowl. Separately, stir the honey into the lukewarm water until dissolved, then whisk in the instant yeast until dissolved. Let the mixture sit for 1 minute, then pour it over the the starter and stir to soften the starter.

Separately, whisk the egg, egg yolks, and vanilla together, then add to the starter mixture and stir until evenly incorporated.

Add the flour and salt. If using a mixer, use the paddle attachment and mix on the lowest speed for 2 minutes. If mixing by hand, stir with a large, sturdy spoon for about 2 minutes. The dough will be coarse, wet, and batterlike; although it will be soft and sticky, it should hold together. Use a wet bowl scraper or spatula to scrape the dough back down into the bowl, if necessary.

Resume mixing on the lowest speed or by hand, gradually adding the sugar in $^1/_2$-tablespoon increments; wait until each addition of sugar has been thoroughly incorporated before adding the next. The dough should now be smoother, though still very soft and sticky. Increase the mixer speed to medium-low or stir by hand more vigorously and mix for 5 minutes to develop the gluten, stopping a few times to scrape down the sides of the bowl and the paddle or spoon.

Switch to the dough hook and mix on medium-low speed or continue mixing by hand, gradually adding the butter in 1-tablespoon (0.5 oz / 14 g) increments; again, waiting until each addition is thoroughly incorporated before adding the next piece. Scrape down the sides of the bowl and the hook or spoon as needed. If using a mixer, you can increase the speed to medium-high to incorporate the butter more quickly. It should take about 5 minutes to work in all of the butter, and at the end the dough should be shiny, soft, sticky if squeezed, and very supple, with a nice pillowlike feel to it when formed into a ball.

Scrape the bowl down and mix on medium speed or by hand for 5 minutes more to fully develop the gluten; you should be able to pull out long, taffylike strands of dough.

Add the dried fruit, then mix on the lowest speed with the dough hook, or by hand, for 1 or 2 minutes to evenly distribute the fruit. If the fruit was soaked overnight, drain off any excess liquid and fold the fruit in by hand. In this case, you may need to add about $3^1/_2$ table-spoons (1 oz / 28.5 g) of bread flour to compensate for the moisture in the fruit.

Use a wet bowl scraper or spatula to transfer the dough to a lightly floured work surface, then dust the top of the dough with flour. Firm up the dough and form it into a smooth ball by stretching and folding it once, as shown on page 18.

Weigh out the desired size of pieces, form them into balls, and place in oiled molds or pans. Depending on the type of bread you're making, the dough will either double or triple in size as it rises. If using a full-size *pandoro* pan or panettone mold, you'll need about 24 ounces (680 g) of dough, which will fill the mold one-third full. If using smaller molds, including popover molds, use however much dough is required to fill each mold one-third full.

Let the panettone rise for 12 hours. You can also refrigerate the dough and bake it anytime during the next 4 days, but the rising time will be quite long, closer to 14 hours.

BAKING

About 15 minutes before baking, preheat the oven to 350°F (177°C). For loaves weighing more than $1^1/_2$ pounds, preheat the oven to 325°F (163°C).

The baking time will vary depending on the size of the panettone, ranging from 30 minutes for smaller shapes to 45 minutes or longer for large loaves. The panettone is done when it is a golden brown on all sides, when the loaf sounds hollow when thumped on the bottom, and when the internal temperature is about 185°F (85°C) in the center. It should still feel slightly soft and tender if squeezed but will firm up as it cools.

Cool in the pan for at least 5 minutes before removing; if baked in paper panettone molds, it isn't necessary to remove the paper. Large panettone should be cooled upside down on a wire rack, and any form of panettone should be cooled thoroughly before serving. Many bakers insist that panettone needs at least 8 to 14 hours of cooling, but 3 hours should be sufficient.

VARIATIONS

If using dried fruit, such as raisins, dried cranberries, or dried cherries, you can simply add them to the dough as directed, or soak them overnight in rum, brandy, or liqueur, using 1 tablespoon (0.5 oz / 14 g) of liqueur for every 3 tablespoons (1 oz/ 28.5 g) of fruit.

You can also make your own soaking syrup by bringing $^1/_2$ cup (4 oz / 113 g) of sugar and $^1/_2$ cup (4 oz / 113 g) of water to a boil to make a simple syrup. When it cools, add 1 teaspoon

(0.16 oz / 4.5 g) of orange or lemon extract, and 1 teaspoon (0.16 oz / 4.5 g) of vanilla and 1 teaspoon (0.16 oz / 4.5 g) of almond extract (optional). Add the fruit to the syrup and let it soak overnight. Another excellent option for flavoring the fruit is Fiori di Sicilia. This wonderfully aromatic and delicious essence that combines vanilla and citrus is available from King Arthur Flour and other suppliers of specialty ingredients.

If you soak the fruit using either of these methods, strain off the the excess liquid, then fold the fruit into the dough by hand, along with about $3\frac{1}{2}$ tablespoons (1 oz / 28.5 g) of extra bread flour.

You can decorate the top of the baked panettone with white fondant glaze (see page 144), or any other glaze that you like.

This recipe makes exquisite brioche as well as holiday bread. For brioche, simply omit the fruit. (See below for instructions on shaping *brioche à tête*.) For an extra treat, top the brioche with streusel (see page 154) before baking. Another option is to use the dough as a tartlet shell and fill it with clafouti, a fruit-filled custard.

Making Brioche à Tête

To shape *brioche à tête*, roll one end of a small ball of dough (typically $1\frac{1}{2}$ to 2 ounces or 42.5 to 56.5 grams) into a cylindrical cone. Poke a hole in the thick end, then slip the tip of the cone through it so that a nub of dough pokes through to make a "head." Transfer the shaped dough to greased brioche molds.

Stollen

Although this is made from the same dough as the panettone, the final proofing time is very different: none! Stollen's origins are attributed to Dresden, Germany, but it is made in many forms and variations throughout Europe. The name refers to baby Jesus' blanket and it is filled with fruit to signify the gifts of the Magi. It can be folded and formed into a crescent shape or simply rolled up into a log. It is usually finished with a brushing of melted butter and heavily dusted with either confectioners' sugar or granulated sugar. My German friends like to age their stollen for weeks before eating it, but I like it best as soon as it cools—it never lasts more than a day, let alone weeks.

Almond paste is a sweet confection made with sugar and ground bitter almonds; when flavored with rose water or treated with other flavorings and food colors it is also known as marzipan. I find it amazingly delicious. It can easily be rolled into a cigar-shaped bead and used as a center core for stollen; the amount is up to you but about 4 ounces (113 g) per small loaf is probably enough.

1 recipe panettone dough (page 163)

2 cups (12 oz / 340 g) dried or candied fruit
(optional; see the variations on page 166 for full details)

2 cups sliced or slivered almonds, lightly toasted,
or 8 ounces (227 g) almond paste or marzipan (optional)

Melted butter, for brushing

Confectioners' sugar or fine granulated sugar, for topping

MAKE THE DOUGH

Make the panettone dough as directed on page 163.

FINISHING THE DOUGH AND SHAPING

Add the optional dried fruit to the dough, then mix on the lowest speed with the hook, or by hand, for 1 or 2 minutes to evenly distribute it. If the fruit was soaked overnight, drain off any excess liquid and fold the fruit in by hand. In this case, you may need to add about 3^1/$_2$ tablespoons (1 oz / 28.5 g) or more of bread flour to compensate for the moisture in the fruit.

Roll the stollen dough around the bead of almond paste.

Use a wet bowl scraper or spatula to transfer the dough to a lightly floured work surface, then dust the top of the dough with flour. Use a rolling pin or your hands to roll out or pat the dough into a 9 by 6-inch rectangle, or divide the dough into two equal portions and roll them into 7 by 5-inch rectangles for smaller loaves. Sprinkle the almonds over the top or place the cigar-shaped bead of almond paste at the end closest to you, then roll the dough up and shape it into a loaf, sealing the crease by pinching the dough with the edge of your hand.

BAKING

Place the stollen on a parchment-lined sheet pan and put the pan in a cold oven. Turn the oven to 350°F (177°C), or 300°F (149°C) for a convection oven.

Bake for 25 minutes (as the oven comes to full temperature), then rotate the pan and bake for another 25 to 35 minutes. The total baking time will depend on the size of the loaf. The stollen is done when it is firm to the touch, sounds hollow when thumped, and is a rich golden brown. It should register 185°F (85°C) in the center. As soon as the stollen comes out of the oven, brush the entire loaf with melted butter, then dust it heavily with confectioners' sugar or roll it in fine granulated sugar to coat.

Cool thoroughly before serving. Many bakers insist that stollens need at least 8 to 14 hours of cooling, but 3 hours should be sufficient.

Greek Christmas or Easter Bread

MAKES 1 LARGE LOAF OR 2 OR MORE SMALL LOAVES

In Greece and Turkey, this bread is called *Christopsomo* or *tsoureki* (also known as *lambprop-somo* during Easter). It differs from stollen in that it's proofed before baking, but the proofing time is shorter than for panettone. Mastic gum, also called mastica, is an aromatic gum resin derived from the bark of a Mediterranean shrub tree in the pistachio family. It can be found at stores that specialize in Greek and Middle Eastern ingredients. It adds a subtle and...... breath-freshening flavor and aroma (no surprise, it has long been used as a natural breath freshener).

1 recipe panettone dough (page 163)
1 teaspoon (0.25 oz / 7 g) ground cinnamon
Pinch of ground nutmeg
Pinch of ground cloves
Pinch of ground allspice
1 teaspoon (0.25 oz / 7 g) mastic gum (optional)
1/2 cup (2 oz / 56.5 g) chopped toasted walnuts or almonds
1 cup (6 oz / 170 g) golden raisins or diced dried apricots, if making Easter bread
1 cup (6 oz / 170 g) dried cranberries or any type of raisins, if making Christmas bread
1 egg plus 1 tablespoon of water, for egg wash
Simple syrup (4 oz / 113 g water and 4 oz / 113 g sugar, brought to a simmer), for glaze (optional)

MAKING THE DOUGH

Make the panettone dough as directed on page 163, whisking the cinnamon, nutmeg, cloves, allspice, and mastic gum into the flour before adding the flour to the dough.

FINISHING THE DOUGH AND SHAPING

Add the nuts and the dried fruit appropriate to the bread you're making, then mix on the lowest speed with the paddle attachment, or by hand, for 1 or 2 minutes to evenly distribute the fruit. If the fruit was soaked overnight, drain off any excess liquid and fold the fruit in by hand. In this case, you may need to add about 3$^1/_2$ tablespoons (1 oz / 28.5 g) of bread flour to compensate for the moisture in the fruit.

Use a wet bowl scraper or spatula to transfer the dough to a lightly floured work surface, then dust the top of the dough with flour. Firm up and form the dough into a smooth ball by stretching and folding it once, as shown on page 18.

For Easter bread, divide the dough into three equal pieces and form them into a braid (see page 97). Traditionally, three hard-boiled eggs, dyed red, are nestled in the braids just before the Easter loaf is baked, but I prefer to add them after the loaf comes out of the oven, so that they retain their bright red color. For Christmas bread, set aside 4 ounces (113 g) of dough, shape the remaining dough into a *boule* (see page 20), and place it on a parchment-lined baking sheet to proof. Divide the reserved dough into two equal pieces, cover them in plastic wrap, and refrigerate. This dough will later be rolled into ropes, which are used to form a cross on top of the bread, alongside the *boule.*

Mist the shaped dough with spray oil and cover loosely, then let the dough rise at room temperature for 90 minutes to 2 hours, until it swells noticeably; the bread will rise further in the oven. You can also refrigerate the dough and bake it anytime during the next 4 days, but the rising time will be quite long.

For Christmas bread, roll out the reserved pieces of dough into two 8-inch ropes, and lay them across the loaf to form a cross (apply the cross to the loaf 30 minutes before baking). You can cut a slit 2 inches long at each end of both ropes with a scissors to split them, and curl the ends for a decorative rose cross. Then apply the egg wash. (If you apply the egg wash first, the cross will slide off.) Easter-style braided loaves can also be egg washed just prior to baking, but this is optional.

BAKING

About 15 minutes before baking, preheat the oven to 325°F (163°C).

Bake for 25 minutes, then rotate the pan and bake for another 35 minutes. The loaf should be golden brown and have an internal temperature of at least 185°F (85°C) in the center. For a shinier loaf, brush the top with hot simple syrup or vegetable oil as soon as it comes out of the oven.

Cool on the pan for at least 5 minutes, then transfer to a wire rack and cool for at least 60 minutes before slicing or serving.

Hot Cross Buns

Hot cross buns are a traditional Good Friday bread, but they can be made anytime (in Elizabe-than England they could only be baked during Easter week or during Christmas, but times have changed). There are, of course, many similar commemorative breads throughout Europe, each with their own twist. Currants and spices such as allspice, mace, nutmeg, and cinnamon are commonly used in the English version. Much folklore and many recipe variations for hot cross buns are available on the Internet (and they're worth reading), but I prefer the following addi-tions to the basic holiday bread recipe. However, feel free to use your own favorite spice and fruit combinations, or simply bake the buns without any additions, as the buns are wonderful with or without the fruit, spices, and glazed cross.

1 recipe panettone dough (page 163)
1³/₄ cups (8 oz / 227 g) currants or raisins (optional)
1 teaspoon (0.25 oz / 7 g) ground cinnamon (optional)
1 teaspoon (0.25 oz / 75 g) ground allspice (optional)
¹/₂ teaspoon (0.13 oz / 7 g) ground nutmeg or mace (optional)
1 egg plus 1 tablespoon water, for egg wash
White fondant glaze (page 144)

MAKING THE DOUGH

Make the panettone dough as directed on page 163.

FINISHING THE DOUGH AND SHAPING

Add the dried fruit and spices to the dough, then mix on the lowest speed with the dough hook, or by hand, for 1 or 2 minutes to evenly distribute the fruit. If the fruit was soaked overnight, drain off any excess liquid and fold the fruit in by hand. In this case, you may need to add about 3¹/₂ tablespoons (1 oz / 28.5 g) of bread flour to compensate for the moisture in the fruit.

Use a wet bowl scraper or spatula to transfer the dough to a lightly floured work surface, then dust the top of the dough with flour. Divide the dough into 2- or 3-ounce (56.5 to 85 g) portions. Shape each into a round roll (see page 25), and place on a parchment-lined baking sheet. Mist the dough with spray oil, cover loosely with plastic wrap, and proof for about 60 minutes, until the dough just begins to swell.

About 15 minutes before baking, preheat the oven to 350°F (177°C). Brush each bun with egg wash just before baking.

Bake for 10 minutes, then rotate the pan and bake for another 8 to 12 minutes. The total baking time will depend on the size of the buns. The buns should be golden brown on all sides and sound hollow when thumped on the bottom, and the internal temperature should be about 185°F (85°C) in the center. The buns will feel slightly soft and tender if squeezed, but will firm up as they cool.

Cool the buns for about 15 minutes, then drizzle or pipe a cross of fondant glaze on top of each bun. Cool for an additional 10 minutes before serving.

The Best Biscuits Ever

I've set myself up by staking a claim to the best biscuits ever. But when I made these biscuits, I was so astonished by their flavor and texture that I decided there couldn't possibly be a more perfect biscuit—at least not any that I've ever tasted. Be forewarned, a generous amount of butter is a key ingredient here, so these biscuits are not for those who are squeamish about fat! That said, if you find these biscuits to be too rich, feel free to use low-fat buttermilk instead of cream for the liquid. Some people insist that only shortening has enough pure fat in it to make a flaky biscuit. While lard and shortening do contain 100 percent fat to butter's mere 85 percent, there's nothing to match butter when it comes to flavor. Also, I find that biscuits made with shortening sometimes have a waxy aftertaste. If you insist on using shortening, chill it for 1 hour before cutting it into the dough, and reduce the amount by about 15 percent, to 7 tablespoons (3.5 oz / 99 g).

I have heard it said that there are two types of people in the world, those who like tender biscuits and those who like flaky biscuits. (I'm usually in the flaky camp.) In this recipe, I've replaced the traditional buttermilk with cream, which essentially makes this both a cream biscuit (and therefore tender) and a flaky biscuit. If you wonder how I arrived at this idea, it was one of those aha/duh moments, in this case brought about because I had forgotten to buy buttermilk. Discovering that I had some heavy cream on hand, I realized that there was no rule prohibiting me from trying to bring the best of both worlds together.

I learned a new trick for incorporating the butter into the flour from a few of my excellent recipe testers: Freeze the butter, then use the large holes on a cheese grater to grate it directly into the dry ingredients (or use the grater attachment on a food processor, with the dry ingredients in the bowl below). Not only does this method save time, but it creates the perfect size butter pieces for the biscuits. You can use this method when making pie dough too!

continued

2 tablespoons (1 oz / 28.5 g) white vinegar, apple cider vinegar, or lemon juice

1 cup (8 oz / 227 g) cold heavy cream

$^{1}/_{2}$ cup (4 oz / 113 g) cold unsalted butter

1 cup (4.5 oz / 128 g) all-purpose flour

$^{3}/_{4}$ cup (3.5 oz / 99 g) pastry flour (if you do not have pastry flour, use all-purpose flour)

1 tablespoon (0.5 oz / 14 g) sugar

$2^{1}/_{4}$ teaspoons (0.5 oz / 14 g) baking powder

$^{1}/_{4}$ teaspoon baking soda

$^{1}/_{2}$ teaspoon (0.13 oz / 3.5 g) salt, or $^{3}/_{4}$ teaspoon coarse kosher salt

DO AHEAD

Stir the vinegar into the cream to acidify it, then refrigerate it to keep it cold. Place the butter in the freezer, for at least 30 minutes, to harden.

Whisk the flours, sugar, baking powder, baking soda, and salt together in a mixing bowl.

Place a cheese grater in or over the bowl of dry ingredients. Remove the butter from the freezer, unwrap it, and grate it through the large holes into the dry ingredients, tossing the butter threads in the flour mixture as you grate to distribute them. (An alternative method is to place the butter on a cutting board, and dust it and the work surface with flour. Cut the butter into $^{1}/_{4}$-inch slices. Dust the slices with flour, stack a few of them up, and cut them into $^{1}/_{4}$-inch strips, then rotate the stack a quarter turn and cut the strips into $^{1}/_{4}$-inch cubes. It's okay if the butter is smaller, such as pea-size. Toss the floured butter bits into the dry ingredients and continue cutting all of the butter in the same manner and adding it to the flour mixture. You can see why I like the grater method better.)

Use your fingertips to separate and distribute the butter pieces evenly, breaking up any clumps but not working the butter so much that it disappears or melts into the flour. Add the cream mixture and stir with a large spoon until all of the flour is hydrated and the dough forms a coarse ball. Add a tiny bit more cream if necessary to bring the dough together.

Transfer the dough to a generously floured work surface, then dust the top of the dough with flour. Working with floured hands, use your palms to press the dough into a rectangle or square about $^{3}/_{4}$ inch thick. Use a metal pastry scraper to lift the dough and dust more flour underneath. Dust the top of the dough with flour as well, then roll it out into a rectangle or square about $^{1}/_{2}$ inch thick. Then, using the pastry scraper to help lift the dough, fold it over on itself in three sections as if folding a letter.

Rotate the dough 90 degrees, then once again lift the dough and dust more flour underneath. Dust the top with flour as well, then once again roll it out into a square or rectangle about $1/2$ inch thick and fold into thirds. Give the dough another quarter turn and repeat this procedure again. Then, repeat one final time (four roll-outs in all).

After the fourth folding, dust under and on top of the dough one final time, then roll the dough out to just under $1/2$ inch thick, in either a rectangle (for triangle- or diamond-shaped biscuits) or an oval (for round biscuits). Use just enough flour to keep the dough from sticking to the work surface.

Cut the biscuits with a floured metal pastry scraper or pizza cutter, or with a floured biscuit cutter for rounds; a 2-inch biscuit cutter will yield 20 to 24 small biscuits. Transfer the biscuits to an ungreased sheet pan (lined with parchment paper or a silicone mat if you like), placing them about $^1/_2$ inch apart.

Let the cut biscuits rest for 15 to 30 minutes before baking to relax the gluten; this will create a more even rise (even better, if you have room, place the pan of biscuits in the refrigerator to chill). If you'd like to bake the biscuits later, see the sidebar on page 180 for make-ahead options.

TO BAKE

About 20 minutes before baking, preheat the oven to 500°F (260°C).

Transfer the biscuits to the oven and lower the oven temperature to 450°F (232°C), or 425°F (218°C) for a convection oven. Bake for 8 minutes, then rotate the pan and bake for another 6 to 10 minutes, until both the tops and the bottoms of the biscuits are a rich golden brown; the baking time will be shorter in a convection oven. The biscuits should rise about $1^1/_2$ times in height.

Place the pan on a wire rack, leaving the biscuits to cool on the hot pan for at least 3 minutes before serving. The biscuits will stay warm for about 20 minutes.

VARIATIONS

These biscuits are perfect without the addition of other ingredients, but it can be fun to enhance them with sweet or savory flavors. Here are four variations. Feel free to create your own versions, using these as examples.

To make cheese biscuits, grate 8 ounces (227 g) of Cheddar or any medium-soft cheese you like, such as Gruyère, Gouda, or Provolone. This will yield about 2 cups of cheese. Each time you fold the dough, sprinkle one-fourth of the cheese over the surface before folding it. This may look like a lot of cheese, but it will melt and almost disappear into the biscuits when you bake them.

To make savory biscuits, layer caramelized onions into the biscuits when you fold them. You'll need to cook the onions well in advance, because it's important that they be cool when you layer them; otherwise, they'll cause the butter in the dough to melt, which will damage the texture of the baked biscuit. To make the onions, slice 2 large white or yellow onions into thin strips. Sauté them over medium heat in 1 tablespoon (0.5 oz / 14 g) of vegetable oil until very soft and translucent. Add 2 tablespoons (1 oz / 28.5 g) of sugar and, optionally, 1 tablespoon (0.5 oz / 14 g) of balsamic vinegar, and continue cooking and stirring until the pan

Keys to a Successful Flaky Biscuit

* The single most important technique is to use very cold butter and liquid. Some biscuit makers go so far as to chill the flour, but this isn't necessary if the butter and cream are cold. Using cold ingredients ensures that the butter stays in bits and pieces, which shortens the gluten strands (thus the term *shortening*, used to describe all solid fats, including butter and margarine). Using bits of cold butter creates weak points in the dough that flake off when you take a bite.

* Work quickly to keep the dough cold, but don't overwork the dough. Gluten is what makes dough tough, and the more you mix the dough, the more organized the gluten strands become. As a general rule of thumb, mix only as long as needed to get the job done. As every great biscuit maker will attest, it's all in the touch.

* The folding technique described in the recipe is similar to the lamination method known as blitz. It creates many thin layers of dough and fat, causing the biscuits to puff up and open like an accordion, creating maximum flakiness.

* The oven must be hot in order to trap the butter inside the biscuit and increase the puffing quality. In a cooler oven, below 450°F (232°C), some of the butter might run out onto the pan, so preheat the oven to 500°F (260°C), then lower the heat to 450°F (232°C) as soon as you put the biscuits in to bake. (If you preheat the oven to 450°F (232°C), it will drop to below 400°F (204°C) when you open the door.)

* Chilling the biscuits before baking them not only relaxes the gluten, it also minimizes the amount of butter that may run out of the biscuits as they bake.

juices thicken into a honeylike syrup and the onions have the consistency of marmalade. This will take 15 to 20 minutes altogether.

To make other savory variations, read on. Seasoned biscuits make a nice accompaniment to eggs, especially if made with fresh herbs. You can use any combination of fresh basil, parsley, dill, chervil, cilantro, or whatever herbs you like. Use about 3/4 cup of fresh herbs, either minced or cut into thin strips. Be careful when using strong herbs or spices, such as rosemary, oregano, sage, anise, fennel, cumin, chili powder, and the like, as they can easily overpower the biscuits. Use these stronger seasonings in moderation and in combination with milder herbs like parsley. Ground pepper is always an option; just $^1/_4$ teaspoon will provide a surprisingly strong kick. Dried herbs will also work, but don't use more than $^1/_4$ cup; and again, use primarily mild herbs like parsley, chervil, and basil.

To make sweet variations, keep in mind that there is very little difference between a biscuit and a scone, so consider sweet biscuits to be flaky, tender scones and try adding dried fruits such as currants, raisins, cranberries, cherries, pineapple, apricots, or blueberries, as well as candied ginger (in moderation). Cut larger dried fruit into small bits. Add 1 cup (6 oz) of dried fruit (or more, if you like) in any combination, when you add the cream. Just don't use fresh fruit or berries, as they would make the biscuits soggy and destroy the flakiness.

Make-Ahead Tips

The best way to make biscuits is to bake them 15 to 30 minutes after the dough is cut, placed on the pan, and briefly chilled. However, when this isn't always practical, it's better to bake the biscuits when you plan to eat them rather than bake them in advance and try to warm them up later. So here are three make-ahead options:

Freeze: Cut and pan the biscuits but don't bake them. Instead, completely wrap the pan (under and around the pan) in plastic wrap or use a food-grade plastic bag. If you wrap it well, you can freeze the pan of unbaked biscuits for up to 1 month. Remove the pan from the freezer at least 3 hours before you plan to bake the biscuits so they can thaw. Don't bake them while they're still frozen or they won't rise or bake evenly. If freezer space is an issue, you can also wrap individual biscuits in plastic wrap, stack them up, and freeze them.

Refrigerate: Wrap the pan or individual biscuits as described above, but instead of freezing, refrigerate them. This is especially practical if you plan to bake the biscuits within 3 days. For even baking, remove the biscuits from the refrigerator about 30 minutes before baking to remove some of the chill.

Parbake: Bake the biscuits as described in the recipe, but only until slightly golden on the tops and bottoms—4 to 5 minutes less than the full baking time. Remove the pan from the oven and cool the biscuits thoroughly before wrapping them individually or wrapping the entire pan and freezing. When you want to finish baking them, preheat the oven to 450°F (232°C) and place the frozen biscuits on an ungreased baking sheet. Bake for 10 to 12 minutes, until the tops and bottoms of the biscuits are golden brown. Cool for 5 minutes before serving; this allows the heat to reach the center, warming but not drying out the biscuit.

Croissants

The dough for croissants, Danish, and certain other pastries is made by a method known as lamination, which involves folding layers of dough and butter (or another fat) to create many thin layers that puff when baked. Puff pastry, the classic unyeasted version of this dough, is used to make many pastries. In this book, I'll stick with a yeasted formula that can be used to make both croissants and Danish pastry.

There are many versions of laminated dough and many systems of rolling to create a specific number of layers. The system I'm presenting here certainly isn't the only one that works, but I like it because it's easy and also incorporates overnight fermentation to create a superb product. Feel free to modify it if you prefer more or fewer layers. The most common error home bakers make when laminating is to apply too much pressure to the dough, which breaks the paper-thin layers of dough and fat. To help with this, the formula here creates a very soft, pliable dough, and the method calls for a fair amount of dusting with flour to prevent sticking.

There are two parts to the final dough: the *détrempe* and the butter block. The *détrempe* is the plain dough before the butter is rolled in. The butter block is the fat that will be laminated between layers of dough. There are many ways to incorporate the fat into the *détrempe*, including spreading it by hand in dabs over the rolled-out dough, which is sometimes called spotting. The method here is more systematic, using a series of letter folds (in thirds) to produce 81 layers of dough and fat—more than enough for a great accordion-style expansion of the layers (one of the recipe testers called it a concertina effect). Should you decide to experiment and try making more layers, just keep in mind that the layers are more vulnerable to rupturing as they get thinner, which defeats the purpose of laminating. I always suggest getting good at 81 layers before adding a fourth letter fold, which will increase the number of layers to 243.

You can use either unbleached bread flour or all-purpose flour for the dough. Bread flour provides more structure, while all-purpose flour, being slightly softer, makes a more tender product.

$4^2/_3$ cups (21 oz / 595 g) unbleached bread or all-purpose flour

$1^3/_4$ teaspoons (0.4 oz / 11 g) salt, or $2^1/_2$ teaspoons coarse kosher salt

$^1/_4$ cup (2 oz / 56.5 g) sugar

1 tablespoon (0.33 oz / 9 g) instant yeast

$^3/_4$ cup plus 2 tablespoons (7 oz / 198 g) cold whole or low-fat milk

1 cup (8 oz / 227 g) cool water (about 65°F or 18°C)

2 tablespoons (1 oz / 28.5 g) unsalted butter, melted
or at room temperature

BUTTER BLOCK

$1^1/_2$ cups (12 oz / 340 g) cold unsalted butter

2 tablespoons (0.57 oz / 16 g) unbleached bread or all-purpose flour

DO AHEAD

To make the *détrempe,* combine the flour, salt, sugar, and yeast in a mixing bowl and whisk to combine. Pour in the milk and water, then add the butter. If using a mixer, use the paddle attachment and mix on the lowest speed for 1 minute. If mixing by hand, use a large spoon and stir for about 1 minute. The dough should be coarse, wet, and shaggy. If it's very wet, like a batter, add a little more flour. If it's firm like regular bread dough or stiff, drizzle in a little more water.

Resume mixing with the paddle attachment on the lowest speed or by hand for another 30 seconds, then increase the speed to medium-high or mix more vigorously for 10 to 15 seconds. The dough will begin to smooth out but should be very soft, supple, and sticky, but not batterlike. Add more flour or water as needed, but mix only until the dough has formed. It is important that it be very soft and pliable, and somewhat sticky. If it's dry to the touch, it needs more water.

Transfer the dough to a lightly floured work surface and, with floured hands, form it into a ball. Place the dough in a clean, lightly oiled bowl, and immediately refrigerate overnight or for up to 2 days.

Leave the *détrempe* in the refrigerator until you're ready to assemble the laminated dough, and make the butter block just prior to incorporating it into the *détrempe*. Cut the cold butter into about 16 pieces and put the pieces in a mixing bowl along with the flour. I recommend using a mixer, as it's so much easier. Use the paddle attachment and mix on the lowest speed for about 1 minute to break down the butter into smaller pieces. Stop the machine and scrape down the bowl and paddle as needed, then mix again until the mixture is no longer lumpy. Increase the speed to medium-high as the butter pieces smooth out, and continue mixing until all of the lumps of butter are gone and you have a smooth paste. (Though it's harder, you can also do this by hand by squeezing the butter and flour for a few minutes until you have a smooth paste. It should be cool to the touch, not warm. You can also use a food processor, but be sure to use pulses rather than running the processor continuously, or the butter may melt.)

Prepare a sheet of parchment paper, waxed paper, or a silicone mat by misting it lightly with spray oil. Use a bowl scraper or spatula to transfer the butter block into a pile in the center of the prepared surface. Mist the top of the butter with spray oil, then cover it with plastic wrap. Press down on the plastic wrap gently but firmly to spread the butter into a 6-inch square (you can also use a rolling pin to lightly tap and roll it into a square). If necessary, lift the plastic wrap and use a metal pastry scraper or bowl scraper to trim off uneven corners or sides, putting the trimmings in the center of the butter block or using them to fill any gaps. The butter block should be about $1/2$ inch thick and smooth across the top, with nicely squared-off corners. If the butter block has warmed up or seems to be melting due to friction or hand warmth, place it in the refrigerator for a few minutes (parchment and all).

To incorporate the butter block into the *détrempe,* clear enough space on the work surface to roll out the dough (eventually) to a width of about 32 inches. Make sure the surface is completely dry, then dust it generously with bread flour or all-purpose flour. Transfer the *détrempe* to the work surface and sprinkle more flour over the top of the dough. Use a rolling pin and, with gentle pressure, roll out the dough to a rectangle about 12$^{1}/_{2}$ inches wide and 6$^{1}/_{2}$ inches long. Always begin by rolling from the center to the four corners, and then roll to the four sides to even it out. Check under the dough frequently, lifting it with a metal pastry scraper to see if it needs more dusting flour. (In addition to preventing sticking, the flour acts like ball bearings, allowing the dough to extend more easily.) Square off the sides and corners of the rectangle with the pastry scraper. The dough will be about $^{1}/_{2}$ inch thick, the same as the butter block.

Lift the parchment with the butter block and set it down atop the dough on the left side to check the sizing. The butter should cover only half of the dough, with just a $^{1}/_{4}$-inch border on the left, top, and bottom. If it covers more than that, remove the butter block and roll out the dough a little wider or taller, as needed. If there's more than $^{1}/_{2}$ inch of dough around the border, shrink the dough by scooting in the edges with the pastry blade or a sturdy ruler.

When the dough and butter are properly matched, remove the plastic wrap and flip the butter block over onto the left half of the dough, again with a border of about $^{1}/_{4}$ inch on the left, top, and bottom. Carefully adjust it into place before removing the parchment. You may need to use the pastry scraper to separate the parchment. If any butter sticks to the parchment, scrape it off and apply it to the top of the butter block, as evenly as possible. Lift the right half of the dough and fold it over the butter block to envelop or sandwich the butter. Stretch the dough along the top rim to seal the butter inside by pressing the top rim of dough to the rim of the underside and pinching them together to create a seal. You now have three layers—dough, butter, dough.

To laminate the dough, lift the dough, one side at a time, and toss more dusting flour underneath it. If the dough sticks to the work surface, use the pastry scraper to break the contact. Lightly dust the top of the dough with flour, then tap the rolling pin over the top of the dough to work out any air bubbles and spread the butter evenly into all four corners. Working from the center to the four corners and then to the four sides, gently roll out the dough into a rectangle, dusting under and on top of the dough with flour as needed. Continue rolling until you have a $^{1}/_{2}$-inch-thick rectangle that's about 16 inches wide and 9 inches long.

Square off the sides and the four corners, then fold the dough as if folding a letter: Fold the right one-third of the dough to the left, and as you lay it down, be sure to square it off so that the top and bottom edges are perfectly aligned with the underlying dough. Then fold the left one-third of the dough to the right in the same way. Use the rolling pin to press out any air pockets so that the folds lay flat, then gently transfer the dough to a lightly floured sheet

INCORPORATING THE BUTTER

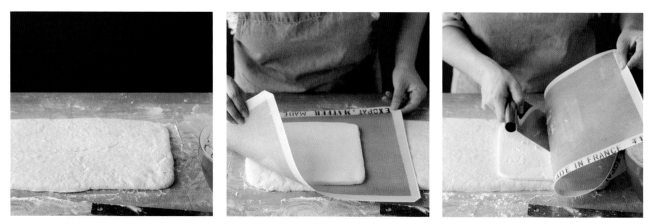

Transfer the butter block to cover half of the dough.

SEAL THE BUTTER INSIDE

Lift and fold the dough to envelop the butter and roll into a rectangle.

LETTER-STYLE FOLD

Fold the dough into thirds, letter-style.

pan and cover loosely with plastic wrap. Let the dough rest at room temperature for 15 to 20 minutes so the gluten can relax. If the butter seems very soft, you can put the pan in the refrigerator for this resting period.

After the resting period, transfer the dough back to the floured work surface with the open seam facing away from you and the closed side facing you. Gently roll out the dough to a rectangle about 16 inches wide by 9 inches long, then once again fold it in thirds. Gently transfer the dough back to the floured sheet pan, cover loosely with plastic wrap, and let the dough rest at room temperature (or in the refrigerator if the butter seems very soft) for 20 minutes.

After the second resting period, once again transfer the dough to the floured work surface, closed side facing you, and gently roll it out and fold it as before. Gently transfer the dough back to the floured pan, cover loosely with plastic wrap, and refrigerate for 20 minutes. You have now completed three "turns" and have created 81 layers of dough and butter.

For the final roll-out and shaping, transfer the dough back to the floured work surface and gently roll it out, first from the center to the corners and then out to the sides, until the dough is just under $^1/_4$ inch thick and forms a rectangle 24 to 28 inches wide and 9 inches long. (If you want to make small croissants or chocolate croissants, roll the dough into a rectangle about 32 inches wide and only about 7 inches long.) Be careful not to put too much downward pressure on the dough as you roll it, or the thin layers could break, but you do need to be somewhat firm, yet patient, as you roll. You may have to stop and dust with flour underneath the dough from time to time or give the dough a short rest if it starts to resist or shrink back. Square off the sides and four corners with the pastry scraper or a ruler.

SHAPING AND BAKING

To make crescent-shaped croissants, begin by cutting out triangles. **For full-size croissants,** cut triangles about 9 inches long by 4 inches wide at the base. (The 9-inch length of the rolled-out dough will shrink to 8 inches as you cut.) Use a ruler or yardstick to measure and, starting at the left side, place a small notch at 4-inch intervals along the bottom edge of the dough with the pastry scraper or a knife. Repeat this along the top edge, but mark the first interval at 2 inches from the left end, then continue measuring at 4-inch intervals from that point on. **For smaller croissants,** roll the dough to only 7 inches long, which means it will be much wider, probably closer to 30 to 33 inches, and make the notches at an interval of only 3 inches, instead of 4 inches.

Use a pizza cutter or a metal pastry scraper to cut a line from the left bottom corner of the dough to the notch in from the left at the top, then simply connect the marks to cut off the dough triangles. When all of the pieces are cut and separated, cut a 1-inch notch into the bottom center of the triangle base of each piece. Spread the bottom as wide as the notch will

allow to create winglike flaps. Start with the flaps and begin rolling up the dough as if it were a rug. Gently pull out the top point (the nose) of the dough as you roll the bottom toward it, but be careful not to squeeze the dough or the layers will break. Stretching the nose will elongate the dough a bit as you roll it up. It should form in either 5 or 7 steps; if you only get 5 steps, you can give the flaps at each end a twist to create another set of steps if you like. Repeat with all of the dough triangles. (If you have any leftover scraps, simply roll them up to make mini croissants or coil them for Danish.)

Place the croissants about 1^1/$_2$ inches apart on a sheet pan lined with parchment paper or a silicone mat, with the nose of each one positioned underneath so that it's anchored. As you pan each croissant, give the end flaps a slight curve inward, facing in the same direction as the nose is pointing, forming a crescent shape. (If you don't want to bake all of the croissants at this time, place the extra croissants on a pan or in individual freezer bags and chill or freeze them.) Cover loosely with plastic wrap and proof at room temperature for $2^1/_2$ to 3 hours. The croissants will rise slowly and swell noticeably in size, but they won't double.

About 20 minutes before baking, preheat the oven to 450°F (232°C). Applying egg wash (see page 135) is an option at this point; some people like the glossy finish it provides, but I don't think it's necessary.

Place the croissants in the oven and lower the oven temperature to 375°F (191°C). Bake for 15 minutes, then rotate the pans and bake for an additional 15 to 20 minutes, until the croissants are a rich golden brown on all sides, without any white sections in the visible layers. If they seem to be baking unevenly or are getting too dark and have streaks of light sections, lower the oven temperature to 325°F (162°C) and extend the baking time as needed. The croissants should feel very light when lifted and be flaky on the surface.

Allow the croissants to cool for at least 45 minutes before serving; an hour is even better. If served while still hot, they'll appear to be greasy because the butter hasn't yet firmed up and been fully absorbed into the pastry.

VARIATIONS

One of the recipe testers accidentally left her melted butter for the *détrempe* on the stove too long and it browned. She used it anyway and reported that it added a wonderful flavor to her finished products. So consider using browned butter in your *détrempe*, but keep a watchful eye on it. Such a small amount of butter can go from brown to black very quickly.

Baking Frozen Croissants

To bake frozen croissants, remove the shaped croissants from the freezer at least 3 hours before you plan to bake so they can thaw. Don't bake them while they're still frozen or they won't rise or bake evenly. Once the croissants have thawed, follow the baking instructions in the recipe.

Chocolate Croissants

You can purchase a product called chocolate batons (available at specialty stores and online) that's specifically designed for rolling into chocolate croissants. But, if you'd like to make your own batons from scratch, here's a recipe, followed by a method for shaping chocolate croissants. You could also fill these croissants with almond paste, or try savory fillings, like ham and cheese, creamed spinach, or bacon crumbles.

1 recipe laminated dough (page 181)

FILLING

6 tablespoons (3 oz / 85 g) cold unsalted butter

2 cups (12 oz / 340 g) semisweet dark chocolate chips or chunks

GARNISH

1 egg, for egg wash

2 tablespoons water, for egg wash

Confectioners' sugar, for garnish (optional)

DO AHEAD

Prepare the laminated dough as directed on page 182, up to the point of shaping and baking. When you get to the final rolling, roll into a rectangle measuring about 32 inches wide by 7 inches high.

SHAPING AND BAKING

To make the filling, melt the butter in a saucepan, then turn the heat down as low as it will go, add the chocolate, and stir until the chocolate is melted. (You can also melt the chocolate and butter together using a double boiler or using a microwave in short bursts.) Pour the chocolate mixture onto a sheet of parchment paper or a silicone mat and use a spatula to spread it into a rectangle about $1/2$ inch thick. Cool until the chocolate is solid; you can put it in the refrigerator to speed this up.

Cut the rolled-out laminated dough into rectangles about $3^1/2$ inches wide and 6 inches long (the 7-inch dough will shrink to 6 inches as you cut it). Use a metal pastry scraper or pizza cutter to cut the cooled chocolate into bars about 3 inches long and $^1/_2$ inch wide. Lay one or two bars across the bottom of each piece of dough, then roll the croissants up into barrel shapes. Place the croissants on a parchment-lined sheet pan about 1$^1/_2$ inches apart, seam side down. Cover loosely with plastic wrap and proof at room temperature for 2$^1/_2$ to 3 hours. (If you don't want to bake all of the croissants at this time, place the extra croissants on a pan or in individual freezer bags and chill or freeze them.) The croissants will rise slowly and swell noticeably in size, but they won't double.

About 20 minutes before baking, preheat the oven to 450°F (232°C). Whisk the egg and water together, the gently brush the egg wash over the croissants.

Place the croissants in the oven and immediately lower the temperature to 375°F (191°C). Bake for 15 minutes, then rotate the pan and bake for an additional 15 to 20 minutes, until the croissants are a rich golden brown on all sides, without any white sections in the visible layers. If they seem to be baking unevenly or are getting too dark and have streaks of light sections, lower the oven temperature to 325°F (162°C) and extend the baking time as needed. The croissants should feel light when lifted and be flaky on the surface.

Cool for at least 1 hour before serving. If you like, you can garnish the croissants after they have cooled with a light dusting of confectioners' sugar tapped through a fine-mesh sieve, or remelt any leftover chocolate filling and apply a squiggle of chocolate to the top.

Danish Pastry

There are dozens of shapes for Danish pastry, far more than I have room to demonstrate, but the shapes below are fundamental and fairly easy to master. (For more shapes, I suggest going to the Web.) The first shape, called *Schnecken* (German for "snail"), is probably the most common shape; with *Schnecken*, you have the option of applying cinnamon sugar to the dough before cutting and shaping. The second shape is a simple pinwheel that's very pretty and popular for serving to guests and on special occasions. I've provided a few recipes for fillings, but you can also use commercial pie fillings (just don't use regular fruit preserves, jams, or jellies because they don't contain starch and aren't oven stable, so they'll melt out of the Danish). I've also provided recipes for two glazes for finishing the Danish and recommend you use both: a hot syrup glaze for shine and retaining freshness, and a simple fondant glaze to accentuate the flavor and provide visual appeal.

1 recipe laminated dough (page 181)

1 egg, for egg wash (optional)

2 tablespoons water, for egg wash (optional)

2 tablespoons (0.75 oz / 21 g) ground cinnamon, for cinnamon sugar (optional)

$1/2$ cup (4 oz / 113 g) sugar, for cinnamon sugar (optional)

1 recipe white fondant glaze (page 144)

HOT GLAZE

$3/4$ cup (6 oz / 170 g) water

$3/4$ cup (3 oz / 85 g) sugar

1 heaping tablespoon apricot preserves (optional)

$1/2$ lemon (optional)

DO AHEAD

Prepare the laminated dough as directed on page 182, up to the point of shaping and baking, and roll out as you would for large croissants, into a rectangle measuring about 24 inches wide by 9 inches long and just under $1/4$ inch thick.

To make *Schnecken,* if you want to use cinnamon sugar, you'll need to apply an egg wash before cutting the dough. Whisk the egg and water together, then gently brush it over the surface of the dough. Separately, whisk the cinnamon into the sugar, then sprinkle the cinnamon sugar over the surface of the dough.

Use a straight edge, such as a sturdy ruler, to cut 1-inch-wide vertical strips, so that you end up with about 24 strips, 8 to 9 inches long (the dough will shrink slightly as you cut it). For large schnecken, use the entire strip; for a mini version, cut each strip in half to make two 4-inch strips. Lift each strip at both ends and twist in opposite directions to form the strip into a springlike coil, then lay the strip on the work surface and coil it in a circular fashion to make a snail shape. (**For full-size** *Schnecken,* you can also coil them from both ends to form either an S-shaped double snail or an eyeglass-shaped double snail, which allows you to fill the schnecken with two fillings.) Tuck the outer end of the coil underneath to close off the circle.

Place the schnecken 1 inch apart on a parchment-lined sheet pan and cover loosely with plastic wrap. Proof at room temperature for 2 to $2^1/_2$ hours, until the dough has swelled noticeably.

To make pinwheels, cut the dough into approximately 3-inch squares for large pinwheels, or $2^1/_2$-inch squares for smaller pinwheels. Working with one piece at a time, use a metal pastry scraper to cut a notch at each corner, cutting from the corner toward the center without connecting the cuts; leave an uncut center about $^1/_2$ inch wide to serve as a platform for the filling. Take the same side of each corner and fold it over to the center, pressing it into the uncut platform. When all 4 corners are folded, use your thumb to press the ends into each other and seal them in the center of the pinwheel. Don't worry if they come apart during the proofing stage; you can press and seal them again before you add the filling.

Place the pinwheels about $^1/_2$ inch apart on a parchment-lined sheet pan and cover loosely with plastic wrap. Proof at room temperature for 2 to $2^1/_2$ hours, until the pieces have swelled noticeably.

BAKING AND GLAZING

About 20 minutes before baking, preheat the oven to 450°F (232°C). Fill the schnecken by using your thumb to make an indent in the center of each coil large and deep enough to hold about 1 heaping teaspoon of filling, then add whatever fillings you like. Fill the pinwheels by pressing the center with your thumb or finger to create a small pocket, and place about 1 teaspoon of whatever fillings you like into the pocket.

continued

For both *Schnecken* and pinwheels, make the fondant glaze while the oven preheats.

Just before baking the Danish, prepare the hot glaze. Combine the water and sugar in a saucepan and bring it to a boil; stir until the sugar is dissolved, then lower the heat to maintain a gentle simmer while the Danish bake. If you like, stir in the apricot preserves, or squeeze the juice from the lemon into the saucepan, then add the entire lemon half.

As the syrup is heating up, place the pan of Danish into the oven and lower the oven temperature to 400°F (204°C). Bake for 6 minutes, then rotate the pan and bake for another 5 to 6 minutes, until a medium golden brown.

As soon as the Danish come out of the oven, brush the hot syrup over them, including over the filling. Let the Danish cool on the pan for about 5 minutes, then drizzle streaks of the fondant glaze over them. Let the glaze set up for about 3 to 5 minutes, then enjoy!

Filling Options

The cream cheese filling can be used by itself or underneath another filling. Although any commercial canned pie filling will work just fine, you can use the fruit filling recipe on page 196 to make it from scratch. The lemon curd can also be used on its own, or as a bed under other fillings. Use the cinnamon butter crumb filling by itself or sprinkle it on top of fruit or cream cheese fillings prior to baking.

CREAM CHEESE FILLING

8 ounces (227 g) cream cheese
2 tablespoons (1 oz / 28.5 g) unsalted butter, at room temperature or melted
6 tablespoons (3 oz / 85 g) sugar
1 egg (1.75 oz / 50 g)
1 teaspoon (0.25 oz / 7 g) vanilla or lemon extract
1³/₄ tablespoons (0.5 oz / 14 g) unbleached all-purpose flour or unbleached bread flour
Pinch of salt

Combine all of the ingredients in a mixing bowl and cream them together until smooth and slightly fluffy. If using a mixer, use the paddle attachment and gradually increase the speed of the mixer to high. If mixing this filling by hand, use a large, sturdy spoon and be

prepared to stir vigorously. The filling should be thick, creamy, and custardlike; it will firm up when baked.

FRUIT FILLING

1 cup fresh or frozen blueberries, pitted cherries, sliced or diced strawberries, or diced apricots, peaches, apples, or pears
$3/4$ cup (6 oz / 170 g) cool water
2 tablespoons (1 oz / 28.5 g) sugar
Pinch of salt
1 tablespoon (0.25 oz / 7 g) cornstarch

If using diced apples or pears, poach them in boiling water for 1 minute, then drain. Whisk the water, sugar, salt, and cornstarch together in a saucepan to make a slurry, then bring it to a boil over a medium heat, stirring constantly. It should thicken by the time it comes to a boil. Remove it from the heat immediately, then stir in the fruit. Some fruits will leach moisture into the slurry, so stir the filling a few times as it cools.

LEMON CURD

6 tablespoons (3 oz / 85 g) lemon juice (fresh is better than bottled)
$1/2$ cup (4 oz / 113 g) sugar
2 eggs (3.5 oz / 99 g), beaten
$1/2$ cup (4 oz / 113 g) unsalted butter, at room temperature, cut into 4 pieces

Whisk the lemon juice, sugar, and eggs together in a double boiler over simmering water, then stir continuously until the mixture begins to thicken; this could take 10 to 15 minutes.

As soon as the mixture thickens, add the butter and stir until it melts. Remove the lemon curd from the heat and continue to stir until the butter is fully incorporated. If it's lumpy, push it through a fine-mesh sieve to smooth it out. Lay a piece of plastic wrap directly on the surface of the curd and set it aside to cool.

CINNAMON BUTTER CRUMB FILLING

$1/4$ cup (2 oz / 56.5 g) unsalted butter, at room temperature	
1 cup (8 oz / 227 g) light brown sugar	
1 teaspoon (0.25 oz / 7 g) ground cinnamon	
$1^3/4$ tablespoons (0.5 oz / 14 g) unbleached all-purpose flour or unbleached bread flour	
Pinch of salt	

This is hard to mix by hand, so I recommend using a mixer. Using the paddle attachment, cream the butter and sugar together on medium-high speed until the butter disappears into the sugar. Add the cinnamon, flour, and salt and mix on low speed until all of the ingredients are evenly distributed.

VARIATION

If you want richer, softer Danish dough, when making the *détrempe*, replace 6 tablespoons (3 oz / 85 g) of the water with 2 eggs (3.5 oz / 99 g).

What's Next for the Artisan Movement?

The growing artisan pizza renaissance that I predicted in 2004 in the pages of *American Pie: My Search for the Perfect Pizza* is, happily, right on schedule. My contention in *American Pie* was that pizza is arguably the most popular food in the world, though not always under that name. After all, pizza is simply dough with something on it, and there are many products that fit the description, from the numerous Italian variations like focaccia, sciattiatta, sfinguini, and even panini to Indian stuffed naan bread, Mexican quesadillas and Central American pupusas, or a simple grilled cheese sandwich—with each incarnation there is something deeply satisfying, almost magical, about the combination of dough and a topping. It doesn't even have to be executed at the highest level—witness the proliferation of frozen pizza products, which, no matter how much they have improved, can never equal a freshly baked pizza from a decent neighborhood pizzeria. Yet, they too are popular and satisfying. I claimed then, and still believe, that there are only two kinds of pizza: good and very good. And by very good, I mean memorable. But, while there are now thousands of very good pizzerias, there were only a handful back in '04 that produced memorable, life-changing pizza (I cited Pizzeria Bianco in Phoenix, Arizona, as the model, with owner Chris Bianco as the reluctant poster boy of this nascent movement).

The current artisan pizza revolution is a wonderful example of our growing hunger for food experiences that are not just good but memorable. We long for experiences that establish new benchmarks in our consciousness, that excite us and make us want to bring our friends and family to share it with us, again and again. We've seen it happen with bread, then the micro beer movement, and more recently with the farmstead cheese movement. Artisanship manifests as the natural and inevitable pendulum swing in a world that has been industrialized and reduced to high-volume processes. Artisanship feeds not only a bodily hunger but

Focaccia (page 57)

also a hunger in our souls, a yearning. This level of quality—the memorable, benchmark kind—is a difficult concept to define, but it's easy to identify when it is encountered. And while it exists in but a small percentage of the foods we consume, it has the power—even in simple, humble peasant foods like bread or pizza—to excite us deeply when we discover it. We will even go on quests in search of it. When I arrive in a city and put out the word that I'm going on a pizza hunt, I have no problem finding fellow pilgrims.

My Recent Pizza Travels

During the months preceding the publication of this book, I had the pleasure of traveling to a number of cities to experience some of the best of the newest American pizzerias. Portland's new artisan pizzerias are all in the same corner of the city, but each serves pizza so good, so different from the others, that each stop seemed like an initiatory experience. **Apizza Scholls** uses medium hydration dough and bakes its large (18-inch diameter) pizzas in a standard Baker's Pride pizza oven, not a wood-fired *forno*. Brian Spangler, the founder and head piz- zaiolo and a former artisan bread baker, cranks his oven up about 100 degrees hotter than most other pizzerias that use the same oven and declares, "It's not about the source of the heat, it's all about the BTUs." His crust is tender and crisp, with a great snap, smoky char spots, and yet a moist, creamy interior. These attributes are hallmarks of artisan pizza, especially when topped with house-made sausage or locally grown and marinated goathorn peppers.

At **Ken's Artisan Pizza**, Ken Forkish uses locally milled Oregon flour and bakes his won- derful, Neapolitan-inspired pizzas in a very hot wood-fired brick oven. He too makes his own fennel sausage and cures his own pancetta. **Tastebud**, owned by Mark Doxtader, just opened in a permanent location after attaining legendary status at Portland farmer's markets for Mark's Montreal-style bagels and rustic pizzas produced in a mobile wood-fire oven on the market site. Tastebud goes for a thicker crust, in the style of Nancy Silverton's groundbreaking **Pizzeria Mozza** in Los Angeles (another place that didn't exist when *American Pie* came out, where the fennel sausage is garnished with a dusting of fennel pollen—now that's what I call artisan gar- nishing!). **Nostrana**, owned by well-known Portland super-chef Cathy Whims, goes for a Naples- style pizza with a thin crust and puffy edge, and intensely flavorful toppings (including, yes, house-cured bacon and locally grown peppers), yet made with American (Oregon milled) flour, not Italian flour.

When I toured the San Francisco area a few days later I discovered a similar Naples-style pizza in Larkspur (just over the Golden Gate Bridge in Marin County) at **Pizzeria Picco**, a wonderful companion to a full-menu restaurant simply called Picco that shares the same space. Chef-owner Bruce Hill's pizza vision is much more a strict homage to the Napoletana method; he uses Caputo "00" flour and an exquisite bright red San Marzano tomato sauce, and bakes his pizzas in a red-hot *forno*. Yet, his creations, including the house-made sausage (of course!) as well as his finely cut *broccoli di ciccio* and a wonderful *baccala* (salt cod) pizza, are distinctly his own and not a Naples copycat.

Craig Stoll, the James Beard Award–winning chef-owner of Restaurant Delfina in San Francisco, now has two locations for his wildly popular **Pizzeria Delfina**. His palate for explosive flavors is similar to Bruce Hill's at Picco and he too serves a *baccala* pizza, yet his crust is dramatically different and, like Apizza Scholls in Portland, is baked with a nice char in gas-fired ovens.

I was also very impressed with the crust and pizzas that came out of the wood-fired oven at **Pizzaiolo**, in Oakland, where chef-owner Charlie Hallowell has realized his long-held vision, born while working the pizza station at Chez Panisse Café under the mentorship of Alice Waters. Five years earlier while attending a pizza class I gave in Berkeley shortly after *American Pie* came out, Charlie told me that he was going to pursue his dream. Again, *baccala* was on the featured pizza—it was a big week for salt cod in the Bay Area and I never tired of it. But I also flipped for the super tender Monterey Bay squid and aioli pizza. Charlie proved that dreams, when fueled by vision and passion, can come true.

The hour-long waits at all of these new spots reflect this fact: If you build it, they will come. And I haven't even mentioned other wonderful places, like **Coalfire Pizza** and **Spacca Napoli**, that I encountered in Chicago, **Pizza Rustica** in Colorado Springs, Marc Vetri's **Osteria** in Philadelphia, or **Una Pizza Napoletana** in New York City, plus about a dozen other places in Manhattan, Brooklyn, and Queens that have recently opened to great acclaim: **Roberta's**, deep in the warehouse district of Bushwick, Brooklyn, as well as **Spunto**, **Co**, **Motorino**, **Franny's**, and **San Marzano** (NYC, as always, is all in). The list goes on and on, and grows daily.

BAKER'S PERCENTAGE FORMULAS

The following formulas express the dough recipes from this book in what are known as baker's percentages, in which all of the ingredients are listed as a ratio against the total flour in the recipe. The totals do not add up to 100 percent because they actually begin with flour as the 100 percent ingredient against which all other ingredients are compared. This system allows experienced bakers to re-create any recipe in any batch size, even without specific weights and measures. A more detailed explanation of the baker's percentage system is given in my book, *The Bread Baker's Apprentice.* You do not need to understand or use this system to make the recipes in this book.

For recipes that use a starter, you will see three tables. One shows the ratios in the starter itself; the second is the mixed dough (with the starter as a separate ingredient in ratio against the flour used in the final dough); and the third is the complete dough formula based on the total flour and other ingredients in both the starter and the final dough. This third table shows the truest picture of the overall ingredient ratios, but some bakers prefer to work with the first tables.

SEED CULTURE	%
Phase 1 (Day 1)	
Whole wheat, whole rye, or unbleached bread flour	100
Unsweetened pineapple juice, filtered water, or spring water	200
Total	300
Phase 2 (Day 3)	
Whole wheat, whole rye, or unbleached bread flour	100
Unsweetened pineapple juice, filtered water, or spring water	100
All of the Phase 1 seed culture	300
Total	500

Phase 3 (Day 4 or later)	%
Whole wheat, whole rye, or unbleached bread flour	100
Filtered or spring water	50
All of the Phase 2 seed culture	250
Total	400
Phase 4 (Day 6 or later)	
Whole wheat, whole rye, or unbleached bread flour	100
Filtered or spring water	33.3
$^1/_2$ cup of the Phase 3 seed culture	133.3
Total	266.6

MOTHER STARTER	%
Whole wheat, whole rye, or unbleached bread flour	100
Filtered or spring water	75
Seed culture	33.3
Total	208.3

LEAN BREAD	%
Unbleached bread flour	100
Salt	2
Instant yeast	0.9
Water	75
Total	177.9

CLASSIC FRENCH BREAD	
Unbleached bread flour	100
Salt	2
Instant yeast	1
Water	66.7
Total	169.7

PAIN À L'ANCIENNE RUSTIC BREAD	
Unbleached bread flour	100
Salt	2
Instant yeast	0.7
Water	80
Olive oil (optional)	2.5
Total	182.7 to 185.7

PAIN À L'ANCIENNE FOCACCIA	
Unbleached bread flour	100
Salt	2
Instant yeast	0.7
Water	80
Olive oil (optional)	2.5
Total	182.7 to 185.7

PAIN AU LEVAIN

Starter

Unbleached bread flour	62.5
whole wheat flour	37.5
Mother starter	31.25
Water	70.5
Total	201.75

Dough

Wild yeast starter	100
Water, lukewarm	68.75
Instant yeast	1.5
Unbleached bread flour	100
Salt	3.75
Total	274

Total dough

Unbleached bread flour	88.25
Whole wheat flour	11.75
Salt	2.3
Instant yeast	1
Water	66
Total	169.3

SAN FRANCISCO SOURDOUGH BREAD	%

Starter

Unbleached bread flour	100
Mother starter	25
Water	62.5
Total	187.5

Dough

Wild yeast starter	75
Unbleached bread flour	100
Salt	3.2
Water	70
Instant yeast (optional)	1.2
Total	249.4

Total dough

Unbleached bread flour	100
Salt	2.1
Instant yeast	0.85
Water	67.5
Total	170.45

NEO-NEOPOLITAN PIZZA DOUGH	%
Unbleached bread flour	100
Salt	2
Instant yeast	0.44
Sugar or honey (optional)	4.2
Water	71
Olive oil (optional)	4.2
Total	177.64 to 181.84

SOURDOUGH PIZZA DOUGH

Starter

Unbleached bread flour	100
Mother starter	25
Water	75
Total	200

Dough

Sourdough starter	44
Water	67
Unbleached bread flour	100
Salt	2.75
Instant yeast	0.6
Sugar, honey, or agave nectar	5.5
Olive oil	5.5
Total	225.35

Total dough

Unbleached bread flour	100
Salt	2.2
Instant yeast	0.47
Sugar, honey, or agave nectar	4.3
Olive oil	4.3
Water	68
Total	179.27

50% WHOLE GRAIN RUSTIC BREAD AND PIZZA DOUGH	%
Whole wheat flour	50
Unbleached bread flour	50
Salt	2
Instant yeast	0.7
Sugar, honey, or agave nectar (optional)	5
Water	80
Olive oil (optional)	5
Total	182.7 to 192.7

100% WHOLE GRAIN RUSTIC BREAD AND PIZZA DOUGH	
Whole wheat flour	100
Salt	2
Instant yeast	0.6
Sugar or honey	6.25
Water	79
Olive oil	6.25
Total	194.1

BAGELS	
Water	56.25
Barley malt syrup, honey, or rice syrup (or diastatic malt powder)	4.7
Instant yeast	0.7
Salt	2.3
Unbleached bread flour	100
Total	163.95

EVERYDAY 100% WHOLE WHEAT SANDWICH BREAD	
Whole wheat flour	100
Salt	1.8
Sugar, brown sugar, honey, or agave nectar	8
Eggs	6.25
Vegetable oil	7
Milk (any kind)	36
Water	36
Instant yeast	1.8
Total	196.85

100% WHOLE WHEAT HEARTH BREAD	
Whole wheat flour	100
Salt	1.8
Honey, agave nectar, brown sugar, or sugar	3.6
Water	78.5
Instant yeast	1.2
Vegetable oil	3.6
Total	188.7

100% WHOLE WHEAT SOURDOUGH HEARTH BREAD

	%
Starter	
Whole wheat flour	100
Mother starter	33.3
Water	75
Total	208.3
Dough	
Whole wheat sourdough starter	78
Water, lukewarm	75
Vegetable oil (optional)	6.25
Whole wheat flour	100
Salt	3.1
Honey or agave nectar, or sugar	6.25
Instant yeast (optional)	1
Total	262.35 to 269.6

Total dough	%
Whole wheat flour	100
Salt	2.2
Honey or agave nectar, or sugar	2.7
Water	74
Instant yeast (optional)	0.7
Vegetable oil (optional)	2.7
Total	179.6 to 182.3

STRUAN

Unbleached bread flour	100
Coarse cornmeal	7
Rolled oats	4.5
Wheat bran or oat bran	3.5
Cooked brown rice	9
Brown sugar	9
Salt	2.9
Instant yeast	2.9
Honey	24.5
Buttermilk or any other milk	18
Water	53
Total	214.3

CHALLAH

Water	53
Instant yeast	1.5
Egg yolks	17.5
Vegetable oil	7.4
Sugar or honey	8.8
Unbleached bread flour	100
Salt	1.9
Vanilla extract (optional)	2.3
Total	190.3 to 192.3

HOAGIE AND CHEESESTEAK ROLLS

	%
Unbleached bread flour	100
Salt	2
Sugar	2
Barley malt syrup (or diastatic malt powder), optional	2
Egg	7.3
Vegetable oil	6.26
Milk (any kind)	21
Water	33
Instant yeast	1
Total	174.85

MANY-SEED BREAD

Unbleached bread flour	88
Whole wheat or whole rye flour	12
Sesame seeds	8
Sunflower seeds	4
Pumpkin seeds	4
Flaxseeds	4
Salt	2.4
Instant yeast	2
Honey or brown sugar	7.8
Buttermilk, any other milk, or yogurt	23.5
Water	47
Total	202.7

SOFT SANDWICH BREAD AND ROLLS

Milk (any kind)	53.5
Instant yeast	1.2
Unbleached bread flour	100
Sugar, honey or agave nectar	10
Salt	1.8
Eggs	6.25
Vegetable oil or unsalted butter	10.7
Total	183.45

SOFT RYE SANDWICH BREAD

Starter	
Rye flour	100
Mother starter	27
Water	86.5
Total	213.5
Dough	
Sour rye starter	64.5
Water	56.25
Molasses	4.2
Vegetable oil	8.3
Instant yeast	1
Unbleached bread flour	100
Salt	2.5
Cocoa powder (optional)	4.2
Total	236.75 to 240.95

Total dough	%
Unbleached bread flour	73
Rye flour	27
Salt	1.8
Instant yeast	0.8
Vegetable oil	6
Molasses	3
Water	62
Cocoa powder (optional)	3
Total	173.6 to 176.6

WILD RICE AND ONION BREAD

Unbleached bread flour	100
Salt	2
Instant yeast	2.4
Cooked wild rice	22
Brown sugar	7.4
Water	44.5
Buttermilk or any other milk	15
Dried minced or chopped onions OR diced fresh onions	3.7 / 30
Total	197 to 223

SOFT CHEESE BREAD

Unbleached bread flour	100
Salt	1.8
Sugar, brown sugar, honey, or agave nectar	8
Water or beer	28.5
Buttermilk or any other milk	32
Instant yeast	1.8
Melted butter or vegetable oil	7
Cheese	43
Fresh onion OR fresh chives, minced (optional)	25 / 3.5
Total	225.6 to 247

CRUSTY CHEESE BREAD

Starter	
Unbleached bread flour	100
Mother starter	33.3
Water	67
Total	200.3
Dough	
Whole or low-fat milk	20
Water or potato water	40
Honey or agave nectar	5
Instant yeast	1.25
Sourdough starter	60
Unbleached bread flour	100
Salt	2.5
Cheese	60
Fresh onion OR fresh chives, minced (optional)	35 / 5
Total	215.75 to 245.75

Total dough	%
Unbleached bread flour	100
Salt	1.8
Instant yeast	0.9
Whole or lowfat milk	14.7
Water or potato water	44
Honey or agave nectar	3.7
Cheese	44
Fresh onion OR	26
fresh chives, minced (optional)	3.7
Total	212.8 to 235.1

ENGLISH MUFFINS

Milk	100
Honey	4.2
Vegetable oil	7
Instant yeast	1.8
Unbleached bread flour	100
Baking soda	0.5
Water	12.5
Salt	1.75
Total	224.4

SOFT PRETZELS

	%
Unbleached bread flour	100
Salt	2
Brown sugar	3.75
Water	60
Instant yeast	0.55
Vegetable oil or melted butter	5
Total	171.35

CRISPY RYE AND SEED CRACKERS

Water	75
Sunflower seeds	18.75
Pumpkin seeds	18.75
Flaxseeds	12.5
Sesame seeds	25
Rye flour	100
Vegetable oil	12.5
Honey or agave nectar	9.4
Salt	0.75
Total	272.65

FLAKY, BUTTERY CRACKERS

Unbleached all-purpose flour	55
Cake flour	45
Salt	2.5
Sugar	5
Baking powder	1.3
Garlic powder	1.3
Vegetable oil or butter	50
Milk	30
Eggs	17.5
Total	207.6

ALL-PURPOSE SWEET DOUGH

	%
Unbleached all-purpose flour	100
Salt	1.8
Sugar	10.7
Whole or low-fat milk	61
Instant yeast	2
Vegetable oil or melted butter	14.25
Total	189.75

CHOCOLATE CINNAMON BABKA

Instant yeast	4.4
Whole or low-fat milk	40
Unsalted butter	20
Sugar	20
Vanilla extract	1.7
Egg yolks	20
Unbleached all-purpose flour	100
Salt	1.7
Total	189.8

PANETTONE

Starter

Unbleached bread flour	100
Mother starter	33.3
Water	66.7
Total	200

Dough

Sourdough starter	124
Instant yeast	1.5
Water	27.5
Honey	10.3
Eggs	24
Egg yolks	31
Vanilla extract	7
Unbleached bread flour or high-gluten flour	100
Salt	2.9
Sugar	20.5
Butter	83
Dried or candied fruit (optional)	110
Total	431.7 to 541.7

Total dough

Unbleached bread flour	100
Salt	1.6
Instant yeast	0.9
Sugar	12
Eggs	14
Egg yolks	17.5
Honey	6
Water	39
Vanilla extract	4
Butter	47
Dried or candied fruit	63
Total	242 to 305

THE BEST BISCUITS EVER

	%
Heavy cream	100
White vinegar	12.5
Unbleached all-purpose flour	56
Pastry flour	44
Sugar	6.25
Baking powder	6.25
Baking soda	0.75
Salt	1.6
Unsalted butter	50
Total	277.35

LAMINATED DOUGH

Détrempe

Unbleached bread flour or all-purpose flour	100
Salt	1.9
Sugar	9.5
Instant yeast	1.6
Whole or low-fat milk	33.3
Water	38
Unsalted butter	4.8

Total dough

Unbleached bread flour or all-purpose flour	100
Salt	1.9
Sugar	9
Instant yeast	1.5
Whole or low-fat milk	32.5
Water	37
Unsalted butter	60
Total	189.1

ACKNOWLEDGMENTS

This is the largest group of people I've ever had to thank. That's because over 500 people volunteered to test these recipes and they provided enormous help. But, before I list them all, I first need to thank the dynamic creative team from Ten Speed Press, including my editor Melissa Moore, copyeditor Jasmine Star, proofreader Linda Bouchard, creative director Nancy Austin, publicist and now managing editor Lisa Regul, and publisher Aaron Wehner, who gets the credit for coming up with the idea for this book. Thanks also to my talented photographer, Leo Gong, his wife Harumi (our hand model and prop stylist, among her many other responsibilities), food stylist Karen Shinto, photo session baking assistants Allen Cohn and Barry Shinto, and our photo session mascot, Samantha, the sweet dachshund puppy who kept us all calm.

Also, thanks to Michael Kalanty and the California Culinary Academy for supplying us with additional baking tools and supplies for the photos, and to the Raphael House for my accommodations in San Francisco during the photo shoot, and to Alan and Katharine Cahn in Portland, Oregon for hosting me and joining in on the Portland pizza hunts.

At home, many thanks to my wife Susan for her superhuman patience, and to my colleagues and superiors at Johnson & Wales University for their support and flexibility: JWU Charlotte campus president, Arthur Gallagher, and chefs Wanda Cropper, Mark Allison, Harry Peemoeller, and Karl Guggenmos; also, Laura Lucille Benoit, proofreader extraordinaire.

A special round of thanks to a few recipe testers who performed over and above the call of duty, including Mark Witt, who set up and hosts our Internet forum and gallery sites that are now a permanent resource for all readers (see page 204 for details); Pamela Schmidt, Lucille Johnston, and Betty Lee who took on the added challenge of extra testing and development on specific projects such as the holiday breads, English muffins, and biscuits. Also, Bruce Gunther, who convinced me to incorporate the stretch and fold method as part of the methodology of this book; I did, and the results improved dramatically! Continual thanks to Debra Wink, for her ongoing sourdough study and suggestions on how to harness those wonderful yet mysterious microorganisms.

As you can see from the following list, there are many others who immersed themselves in the task of helping to create this innovative method of bread making. Some stayed with the project for the entire nine months of testing, while others came in during the middle or at the end with fresh eyes. Believe me, you are all appreciated and you should know that I never could have completed this book without your help and support. It has truly been a collaborative effort! (If I have inadvertently left anyone off this list, I apologize in advance—I never thought there would be so many of you!)

Paul Aboud, Kasra Adjari, Dennis Allison, Ana Alonso, Brian Amos, Kasi Anderson, Matthew Arney, Betsy Arnold, Deb Arsenault, Greg Askew, Elias Barajas, Nicholas Barengo, Greg Baumann, Paul Bear, Matt Behm, Rick Behrens, Kevin Bell, Todd Bennett, Jane Benoit, Laura Lucille Benoit, Dov Berger, Joe Bernardello, Stefan Bert, David Bishop, Hanna Bjonstad, Mark Black, Barb Blackmore, Mary Blender, Anne Bloomer, Karen Blumberg, Emily Blumenthal, Dan Bode, Ruth Boehler, Jennifer Bourassa, Jim Bradley, Marcia Branscom, Benjamin Brenner, Stephanie Brim, Robert Bristow, Broc Brockway, Elizabeth Broderick, Royal Brooks, Dan Brosemer, Jeanie Brown, Try, Nong, and Caterina Brown, Chris Bryan, Claire Bucholz, Kathryn Bundy, Becky Burdashaw, Joseph Burgo, Samantha Butler, Jean Buttimer, Myra Callahan, Jane M. Campbell, Patrick Campbell-Preston, Bryan Carmenti, Bill Carrera, Vicki Carson, Elizabeth Carswell, Mary Cassidy, Sarah Chatfield, Laura Chan, Karen Chen, Sophia Chen, Don Choate, Larry Clark, Carmen Clemons, Richard Clark, Isabelle Cloutier, Jenny Cochran, Mark Cohen, Patti Colbourne, Darren Coleman, Matthew Colflesh, Sikway Condon, Mike Connolly, Jim Cook, Renee Cook, Margaret Cope, David Coppes, Robin Cosby, Barbara Coughlin, Cecil Coupe, Lionel Crews, Amber Crowder, Allison Dale, Nicola Dalheim, Deborah Dana, Chahira Daoud, Don Daugherty, Laurie Davidson, Nat Davidson, Jim Davies, Krek Dayam, Simone DeKleermaeker, Dawn DeMeo, Patrick Dennis, Art Denys, Kathy Destadio, Leandro DiLorenzo, Phyl Divine, Nancy DeVries, Eric Dickey, Brian Dodds, Caroline Donnelly, Judy Donovan, Jim Doubler, Cindi DuMond, Tommi Dungan, Dawn Durham, Laura Dutzi, HopeAllyson Dwiggins, Anita Dwyer, Roxanne, Eberle, Donna Eckert, Barbara Edwards, Jeff Elder, Adam Elhardt, Tim Elliott, Harlow Emilie, Dawn Endico, Deb Estes, Aaron Fabun, Allie Faden, Kevin Falcone, Kevin Farnsworth, Brad Feagins, Cheryl Sutton Fergusan, Victoria Filippi, Paula Finestone, Julie Fiscko, Judy Fitz, Floyd Foess, Alice Forsell, Will Fortin, Marie Fowler, Ryan Fowler, Susan Fox, Paul Friedman, Hans Fugal, Tom Garbacik, Jefferson Garn, Joann Gay, Brian Geiger, Julie Gerstemeier, Tom Giambra, Lara Gibb, Jeff Gicklhorn, Stanley Ginsberg, Chris Glenn, Kathryn Gohl, Simon Goldbroch, Jeff Goldstein, Ofelia Gonzalez, Shari Goodwin, Rosalyn Gorski, Jim Gray, Courtney Green, Kathy Green, Richard Greenhaw, Joe Guiditta, David Gunderson, Thomas Gunn, Bruce Gunther, Michael Gunter, Michelle Gusic.

Dan Haggarty, Lindsey Hair, Tyler Hall, Jutta Hanke, Karen Hanlon, G. Hanna, Eric Hanner, Becky Hart, Tammy Hart, Jack Hattaway, Miriam Hawbaker, Brandi Headon, Frank Healy, Marc Hedlund, Carol Heinen, Dulcey Heller, Natalie Heller, Dougal Hendry, Ellen Herman, Hilary Hertzoff, Jan Hickey, Kathy High, Beth Hinkle, Eric Hohenschuh, Clayton Holland, Frances Holly, Justin Holmes, Kendra Holtz, Jennifer Honnell, Shayda Hoover, Elizabeth Hopkins, Kimberley Horelik, J. Andrew Hubbard, Rick Hullinger. Nilda Incatasciato, Carol Jackson, Sarah Jackson, Andrew Janjigian, Joanne Johnson, Jen Johnston, Lucille Johnston, Raina Joines, Gretchen Jones, Stephen Jones, Tanna Jones, Vincent Jorgenson, Robin Josephs, Stephen Judge, Richard Kairer, Canan Karatekin, Kristen Kasmire, Mary Kasprzak, Shari Katz, Sandra Kavital, Jonathan Keane, Matthew Kerr, Christopher Kessinger, Michael Kelly, Jess Kelly-Landes, Claire Kenney, Christopher Key, Jongjin Kim, John Kino, Sandra Kisner, Logan Kistler, Tami Knight, Eric Kniffen, Trish Kobialka, Zorra Kochtopf, Kristine Konrad, Bob Koontz, Brett Kosinski, Tom Kovalcik, Carol Kowalski, Chris Kridakorn-Odbratt, Malcolm Kronby, Rafi Kruse, Dwayne Kryger, Charles Kutler, Celina Laaksonen, Suzanne Lansford, David LaPuma, Cameron Larios, Natalie Lau, Kelly Lawless, Cameron Lawrence, Wade Lawrence, Bonnie Leach, Bethany Lee, Betty Lee, Dorothy Lee, Gary Lee, Jee-Sun Lee, Justin LeFebvre, Jonathan Leffert, Jacqueline Leung, Sarah Lenz, Melissa LeRay,

Helen LeVann, Elizabeth Lindsay, Caroline Lazuli, Adeline Lim, Noel Llopis, John Llyod-Jones, Jay Lofstead, Bruce Lorenz, Tiffany Low, Gary Lubb, Troy Lubbers, Ed Lyon, Annie MacDonald, Dave MacKenzie, Rick, Mack, Kathleen Madsen, Sharon Maher, Hillie Mailhiot, Tony Malerich, Kathleen Marcozzi, Gina Martin, Penny Martin, Vernon Mauery, Sheila Mayer, Kurt McAdams, David McAtee, Chip McCarthy, Kelly McDonald, Sabine McElrath, Donna McFarren, Rod McLean, Micha McNerney, Chris Meeusen, Paige Meier, Stephen Meier, Claire Meneely, Arte Miastkowski, Bill Middeke, Theresa Miller, Greg Milliser, Lisa Mohen, Kirsty Molnar, Kathy Moore, Derrick Moreno, Kim Morgan, Roxanne Morgan, Neil Morganstern, Tori Mirkemo, Suzy Morris, Moss, Carl Mueller, Robert Mullins, Lindsay Murphy, Clark Murray, Pat Muth, Renae Myers, Jonathan Nacht, Cassandra Nelson, J.R. Nelson, Anja Neudert, Gina Newby, Steve Newell, Phan Ngauv, Laura Nicoletti, Naomi Nishimura, Brian Nivens, Mike Nolen, Bill Nonnemacher, Kevin Noordhoek, Michelle Morris, Jen Norton, G. Travis Norvell, Bob Nowacki, Wendy Nowell, Erin O'Brien, Renee O'Brien, Todd O'Connor, Stephen Odaniell, Myra Orlen, Page Orloff, Sharon Palmer, Andy Parker, Thomas Passin, Laurel Pavesi, Liz Pearson, Marcella Peek, Mandy Peltier, Charles Perry, Michael Peterson, Tina Petok, Emily Phillips, Gail Phillips, Nichole Phillips, Summer Plum, John Plummer, Peter Plummer, Sarah Pokorski, Jessica Polito, Tatiana Popov, Ruth Porter, Barbara Potter, William Powell, Sarah Pratt, Carolyn Price, Deena Prichep, Sherane Prish, Allyson Quibbel, Carla Quinn, Deborah Racine, Michael Ramirez, James Randall, Shannon Rause, Linda Rawson, Evelyn Mae Raymond.

Matthew Ream, Gale Reeves, Sarah Reichers-Krippner, Stephanie Reinhardt, Libby Reiser, Jim Richards, Chuck Robinson, Mike Rodgers, Elaine Rosenfield, Tamar Rudavsky, Laurel Ruma, Eric Rusch, Oliver Rutherford, Peter Ryan, Ryan Sandler, Brian Sands, Corrine Sandusky, Katrina Sarson, Heather Scharbach, Kathleen Scarvie, Eva Schatz, Chrissie Schicktanz, David Schiffrin, Kimberley Schlinke, Lisa Schlunegar, Pamela Schmidt, Chaya Schneider, Jack Scholkoff, Avi Schwartz, Cora Sedlacek, Stephanie Severson, Tom Shaefges, Laura Shaw, Nolan Shaw, Jeff Shields, Beth Sheresh, Lisa Sherman, Mike Shimpock, Adam Shopis, Boaz Shuval, Ryan Simmons, Mike Simpson, Ken Siskind, Sharon Skoglund, Joseph Sloan, Shalisa Smith, Jill Smith-Mott, Nick Smolinske, Arlene Spike, Jaya Srikrishnan, Steve Stanley, Chantal Stark, Anna Stefos, Anita Stebbing, Karen Stewart, Holly Stockley, Esther Stokes, Lynee Stokes, Linda Stoodley, Pam Stowe, Rachel Strange, Ryan Street, Peter Strzebniok, Alison Sue, Betty Sullivan, Jia Sung, Brian Surowiec, Devlyn Swenson, Joseph Szabo, Laura Tabacca, Laura Tanner, Anastasia Tapsieva, James Tatlow, Lewis Skip Taylor, Susan Tenney, Patty-Leigh Theilmann, Stephanie Thomas, Linnea Thomasen, Carolyn Thompson, Mary Tinkham, Matthew Todd, Chuck Toporek, Nathaniel Towery, Robert Traino, August Trometer, Gabriel Trout, Laura Troyer, Candy Tsiao, Zach Tuttle, Celeste Uzee, Jan Willem VanEck, Renee VanHoy, Jason Venkiteswan, Michael Vilalbo, Lisa Volker, Christina Wagenet, Marla Walker, Stewart Walton, Beverly Wang, Gail Wang, Kevin Wang, Lucinda Ward, Doug Washington, Andrew Weber, Lois Wegfahrt, Paul Weeks, Jenny West, Ulrike Westphal, Donna Whitlinger, Mike Wiacek, Rynda Wilk, Jim Wilkinson-Ray, Lori Willingham, Jim Wills, Jean Withnell, Mark Witt, Carla Wolf, Wee Wong, Matthew Wood, Denise Woodward, Steve Wozencroft, Kelly Wright, Kate Wrightson, Lucille Yackoski, Rita Yaezel, Mike Yetter, Shuang Yang, Berta York, Andrew Zajac, Vladimir Zelevinsky, Michael Zemyan, Adam Zerwick, Michael Zhuravel.

OTHER BOOKS FROM PETER REINHART

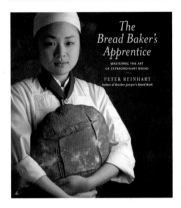

The Bread Baker's Apprentice
Mastering the Art of Extraordinary Bread

9 x 10 inches, 320 pages, full color
ISBN 978-1-58008-268-6
$35.00 hardcover
2002 James Beard Cookbook of the Year
2002 IACP Cookbook of the Year

American Pie
My Search for the Perfect Pizza

7 x 9 inches, 272 pages, two color
ISBN 978-1-58008-422-2
$27.95 hardcover

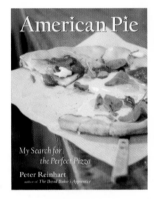

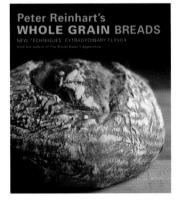

Peter Reinhart's Whole Grain Breads
New Techniques, Extraordinary Flavors

9 x 10 inches, 320 pages, full color
ISBN 978-1-58008-759-9
$35.00 hardcover
2008 James Beard Award Winner

Crust and Crumb
Master Formulas for Serious Bread Bakers

8 x 9⅞ inches, 224 pages, two color
ISBN 978-1-58008-802-2
$19.95 paper
1998 James Beard Award Winner

Available from your local bookstore,
or order direct from the publisher:
www.tenspeed.com